The History of the

FIVE INDIAN NATIONS

Depending on the Province

of New-York in America.

BY

CADWALLADER COLDEN.

Cornell Paperbacks

CORNELL UNIVERSITY PRESS

ITHACA AND LONDON

This book consists of Part I (1727) and Part II (1747) of *The History of the Five Indian Nations*, by Cadwallader Colden. The text is reprinted (with few changes other than romanization of much of the italics, omission of beginning quotation marks except at the opening of a quoted sentence or paragraph, and the correction of some obvious typographical errors) from the 1866 reprinting of the 1727 edition of Part I and from the 1747 edition of Part II.

CORNELL UNIVERSITY PRESS
First printing, Great Seal Books, 1958
Second printing, Cornell Paperbacks, 1964
Eighth printing, 1988

The paper in this book is acid-free and meets the guidelines for permanence and durability of the Committee on Production Guidelines for Book Longevity of the Council on Library Resources.

International Standard Book Number 0-8014-9086-3
PRINTED IN THE UNITED STATES OF AMERICA

To His Excellency

WILLIAM BURNET, *Esq;*

*Captain General and Governor in Chief of
the Provinces of New-York, New-Jersey, and
Territories thereon depending, in America,
and Vice-Admiral of the same, &c.*

SIR;

The Indian Affairs of this Province have appear'd to your Excellency of such Importance to the Wellfare of the People here, that you have carefully apply'd your Thoughts to them, in which I hope your Excellency will have such Success, that not only the present Generation shall enjoy the Benefit of your Care, but our latest Posterity likewise may bless your Memory under their Happiness, the Foundation of which may be laid under your Excellency's Administration, if the People here, who's Interest is chiefly concern'd, do on their parts second your Endeavours, as their Duty requires, towards securing the Peace and advancing the Prosperity of their Country.

The following Account of the Five Nations will show what Dangerous Neighbours the Indians have been, what Pains a Neighbouring Colony (who's Interest is Opposit to ours) has taken to withdraw their Affections from Us, and how dreadful the Consequences may be, if that Colony should succeed in their Designs: and therefore how much we ought to be on our Guard. If we only consider the Riches which a People, who have been and may again be our Enemies, receive from the Indian Trade (tho' we were under no apprehensions from the Indians themselves) it may be thought imprudent in Us to suffer such People to grow Rich and Powerful, while it is in our Power to prevent it, with much less Charge and Trouble than it is in theirs to accomplish their designs.

These Considerations are sufficient to make the Indian Affairs deserve the most serious Thoughts of the Governor of New-York. But I know your Excellency's Views are not confin'd to the Interest of your own Country only.

The Five Nations are a poor Barbarous People, under the darkest Ignorance, and yet a bright and noble Genius shines thro' these black Clouds. None of the greatest Roman Hero's have discovered a greater Love to their Country, or a greater Contempt of Death than these Barbarians have done, when Life and Liberty came in Competition: Indeed, I think our Indians have out-done the Romans in this particular; for some of the greatest Romans have Murder'd themselves to avoid Shame or Torments, (a) Whereas our Indians have refused to Dye meanly with the least Pain, when they thought their Country's Honour would be at stake, by it, but gave their Bodies willingly up to the most cruel Torments of their Enemies, to shew, that the Five Nations consisted of Men whose Courage and Resolution could not be shaken. They sully, however, these noble Vertues by that cruel Passion Revenge, which they think not only lawful, but Honourable to exert without Mercy on their Country's Enemies, and for this only they deserve the Name of Barbarians.

But what have we Christians done to make them better? Alas! we have reason to be ashamed, that these Infidels, by our Conversation and Neighbourhood, are become worse than they were before they knew us. Instead of Vertues we have only taught them Vices, that they were entirely free of before that time. The narrow Views of private Interest have occa-

(a) This will appear by several Instances in the second Part of this History.

sioned this, and will occasion greater, even Publick Mischiefs, if the Governors of the People do not, like true Patriots, exert themselves, and put a stop to these growing Evils. If these Practices be winked at, instead of faithful Friends that have Manfully fought our Battles for us, the Five Nations will become faithless Thieves and Robbers, and joyn with every Enemy that can give them the hopes of Plunder.

If care were taken to plant in them, and cultivate that general Benevolence to Mankind, which is the true Principle of Vertue, it would effectually eradicate those horrid Vices occasioned by their Unbounded Revenge; and then the Five Nations would no longer deserve the name of Barbarians, but would become a People whose Friendship might add Honour to the British Nation, tho' they be now too generally despised.

The Greeks & Romans, once as much Barbarians as our Indians now are, deified the Hero's that first taught them the Vertues, from whence the Grandeur of those Renowned Nations wholly proceeded; but a good Man will feel more real Satisfaction and Pleasure from the Sense of having any way forwarded the Civilizing of Barbarous Nations, or of having Multiplied the Number of good Men, than from the fondest hopes of such extravagant Honour.

These Considerations, I believe, would make your Excellency think a good History of the Five Nations worthy of your Patronage. As to this, I only hope, that you will look on my offering the following Account, however meanly perform'd, to proceed from the Desire I have of making some Publick Profession of that Gratitude, which is so much the Duty of

SIR,

Your Most Obliged

And Most Obedient

Humble Servant,

Cadwallader Colden.

The Preface.

THOUGH every one that is in the least acquainted with the Affairs of North-America, knows of what Consequence the Indians, commonly known to the people of New-York by the Name of the Five Nations, are both in Peace and War, I know of no Accounts of them Published in English, but what are meer Translations of French Authors. This seems to throw some Reflection on the Inhabitants of this Province, as if we wanted Curiosity to enquire into our own Affairs, and that we were willing to rest satisfied with the Accounts the French give us of our own Indians, notwithstanding that the French in Canada are always in a different Interest, and sometimes in open Hostility with us. This Consideration, I hope, will justify my attempting to write an History of the Five Nations at this time; and my endeavouring to remove that Blame with which we may be charged, perhaps will attone for many Faults which the want of Capacity may have occasioned.

Having had the Perusal of the Minutes of the Commissioners for Indian Affairs, I have been enabled to collect many Materials for this History, which are not to be found any where else: And this Collection will, at least, be useful to any Person of more Capacity, who shall afterwards undertake this Task. When a History of these Nations shall be well wrote, it will be of great use to all the British Colonies in North-America; for it may enable them to learn Experience at the Expence of others; and if I can contribute anything to so good a Purpose, I shall not think my Labour lost.

It will be necessary to Excuse two things in the following Performance, which, I am afraid, will be found fault with by those that are the best Judges. The First is, My filling up so great part of the Work with the Adventures of small Parties, and sometimes with those of one single Man. The Second is, The inserting so many Speeches at length. I must confess, that I have done both these designedly.

As to the First, The History of Indians would be very lame without an Account of these Private Adventures; for their War-like Expeditions are almost always carried on by Surprizing each other, and their whole Art of War consists in managing small Parties. The whole Country being one continued Forrest, gives great Advantages to these Sculking Parties, and has obliged the Christians to imitate the Indians in this Method of making War. I believ'd likewise, that some would be curious to know the Manners and Customs of the Indians, in their Publick Treaties especially, who could not be satisfied without taking Notice of several minute Circumstances, and some things otherwise of no Consequence. We are fond of searching into Remote Antiquity, to know the Manners of our Earliest Progenitors: if I be not mistaken, the Indians are living Images of them.

My Design in the Second was, That thereby the Genius of the Indians might better appear. An Historian may paint Mens Actions in lively Colours, or in faint Shades, as he likes best, and in both cases preserve a perfect Likeness: But it will be a difficult Task to show the Wit, and Judgment, and Art, and Simplicity, and Ignorance of the several Parties, managing a Treaty, in other Words than their own. As to my part, I thought myself uncapable of doing it, without depriving the judicious Observer of the Opportunity of discovering much of the Indian Genius, by my Contracting or Paraphrasing their Harrangues, and without committing often gross Mistakes. For, on these Occasions, a skilful Manager often talks Confusedly and Obscurely with design; which if an Historian should endeavour to amend, the Reader would receive the History in a false Light.

The Reader will find a great Difference between some of the Speeches made at Albany, and those taken from the French Authors. The first are genuine, and truly related, as delivered by the Sworn Interpreters, and where Truth only is required; a rough Stile with it, is preferable to Eloquence without it. But I must own, that I suspect our Interpreters may not have done Justice to the Indian Eloquence. For, the Indians having but few words, and few complex Ideas, use many Metaphors in their Discourse, which interpreted by an hesitating Tongue, may appear mean, and strike our Imagination faintly, but under the Pen of a skilful Interpreter may strongly move our Passions by their lively Images. I have heard an old Indian Sachem speak with much Vivacity and Elocution, so that the Speaker pleas'd and moved the Auditors with the manner of delivering his Discourse; which, however, as it came from the Interpreter, disappointed us in our Expectations. After the Speaker had employ'd a considerable time in Haranguing with much Elocution, the Interpreter often explained the whole by one single Sentence. I believe the Speaker in that time imbellished and coloured his Figures, that they might have their full force on the Imagination, while the Interpreter contented himself with the Sense, in as few words as it could be exprest.

He that first writes the History of Matters which are not generally known, ought to avoid, as much as possible, to make the Evidence of the Truth depend entirely on his own Veracity and Judgment: For this reason I have often related several Transactions in the Words of the Registers. When this is once done, he that shall write afterwards need not act with so much Caution.

The History of Indians well wrote, would give an agreeable Amusement to many, every one might find something therein suited to his own Pallat; but even then, every Line would not please every Man; on the contrary, one will praise what another condemns, and one desires to know what another thinks not worth the Trouble of Reading: And therefore, I think, it is better to run the Risque of being sometimes Tedious, than to omit anything that may be Useful.

I have sometimes thought that the Histories wrote with all the Delicacy of a fine Romance, are like French Dishes, more agreeable to the Pallat than the Stomach, and less wholsom than more common and courser Dyet.

An Historian's Views must be various and extensive, and the History of different People and different Ages, requires different Rules, and often different Abilities to write it: I hope, therefore, the Reader will receive this first Attempt of the kind, in this Country, with more than usually Favourable Allowances.

The Inhabitants of New-York have been much more concern'd in the Transactions which followed the year 1688, than in those which preceeded that year. As it requires uncommon Courage and Resolution to engage willingly in the Wars of Cruel and Barbarous Enemies; I should be sorry to forget any that may deserve to be remembred by their Country with gratitude. The First Part of this History going abroad by it self, may give those that have any Memoirs of their Friends who have distinguished themselves, an opportunity of Communicating them, and may thereby enable the Writer hereof to do some Justice to their Merit.

They likewise that are better acquainted with the Indian Affairs may, perhaps, find some Mistakes in what is now Published, and may know some things which I know not, if they will be so kind as to Communicate them, I shall gladly Amend and Insert them in what is to follow.

C. C.

A short Vocabulary of some Words and Names used by the French Authors, which are not generally understood by the English that understand the French Language, and may therefore be Useful to those that intend to read the French Accounts, or compare them with the Accounts now Published.

Names used by the French.	*The same are called by the English or Five Nations.*
ABENAGUIES,	OWENAGUNGAS, or New-England Indians, and are sometimes called the Eastern-Indians.
ALGONKINS,	ADIRONDACKS,
AMIHOUIS,	DIONONDADIES or TUINUNDA-DEKS, a Branch or Tribe of the Quatoghies.
ANIEZ,	MOHAWKS, called Maquas by the Dutch living in the Province of New-York.
BAY des PUANS,	ENITAJICHE.
CHYGAGON,	CONERAGHIK,
CORLAER ou CORLARD,	SCHENECTADY. But the Five Nations generally call the Governor of New-York by this Name, and they often like wise comprehend under it the People of this Province.

Names used by the French.	*The same are called by the English or Five Nations.*
DE-TROIT,	TEUCHSAGRONDIE,
HURONS,	QUATOGHE. But the French now generally call those of that Nation only Hurons, who live at Missilimaki-nack, and who are called Diononda-diks ronoon by the Five Nations.
ILINOIS,	CHICTAGHIKS,
IROQUOIS,	The FIVE NATIONS,
LAC HURON	CANIATARE QUATOGHe or Qua-toghe Lake.
LOUPS,	SCAKHOOK INDIANS.
MANHATTAN,	NEW-YORK. The Island on which the City stands was called Manhattan by the Indians, and still retains that Name with the old Dutch Inhabit-ants.
MASCOUTECS,	ODISTASTAGHEKS,
MAURIGANS,	MAHIKANDER, or River-Indians
MIAMIES,	TWIHTWIES.
MICHILIMAKINAK, ou MISSILIMAKINAK,	TEIADONDORAGHIE.
MISSISAKES,	ACHSISAGHEKS.
NADOUESSIAUX,	NADUISSEKS.
ONEYOUTS,	ONEYDOES.
ONNONTIO,	YONNONDIO, The Name given to the Governor of Canada by the Five Nations.
ONTARIO LAC,	CADARACKUI LAKE,
ORANGE,	ALBANY. The Dutch of this Province call this place Fort Orange to this Day, being the Name given to it by the Hollanders when they possessed this Country.

Names used by the French.	*The same are called by the English or Five Nations.*
OUTAGAMIES,	Under this Name the French comprehend the Quaksies and Scunksiks.
OUTAWAES,	UTAWAWAS or Wagunhas, and sometimes Necariages, the English generally comprehend under the name Utawawas all the Nations living near Missilimakinak.
RENARDS,	QUAKSIES,
SAUTEURS,	ESTIAGHIKS,
SHAOUONONS,	SATANAS,
TATERAS,	TODERIKS,
TERRE ROUGE,	SCUNKSIKS,
TONGORIAS,	ERIGEKS,
TSONONTOUANS.	SENNEKAS.

N. B. The Five Nations, as they have severally a Different Dialect, use different Terminations, and the French generally distinguish that Sound in the Indian Language by (*t*) which the English do by (*d*) but I have neglected such small Differences.

A Short View of the Form of Government of the Five Nations.

IT is necessary to know something of the Form of Government of the People whose History one reads. A few words will serve to give the Reader a general Notion of that of the Five Nations, because it still remains under Original Simplicity, free from those complicated Contrivances which have become necessary to those Nations where Deceit and Cunning have increased as much as their Knowledge and Wisdom.

The Five Nations (as their Name denotes) consist of so many Tribes or Nations joyn'd together by a League or Confederacy, like the United Provinces, without any Superiority of any one over the other. This Union has continued so long that the Christians know nothing of the Original of it.

They are known to the English under the Names of Mohawks, Oneydoes, Onnondagas, Cayugas and Sennekas; but it is probable that this Union at first consisted only of three Nations, *viz.* the Mohawks, Onnondagas and Sennekas, and that the Oneydoes and Cayugas were afterwards adopted or received into this League; for the Oneydoes acknowledge the Mohawks to be their Fathers, as the Cayugas do the Sennekas to be theirs.

Each of the Nations are distinguished into 3 Tribes or Families, who distinguish themselves by three different sorts of Arms or Ensigns, *viz.* the Tortoise, the Bear & the Wolfe. The Sachems of these Families, when they sign any Publick Papers, put the Mark or Ensign of their Family to it.

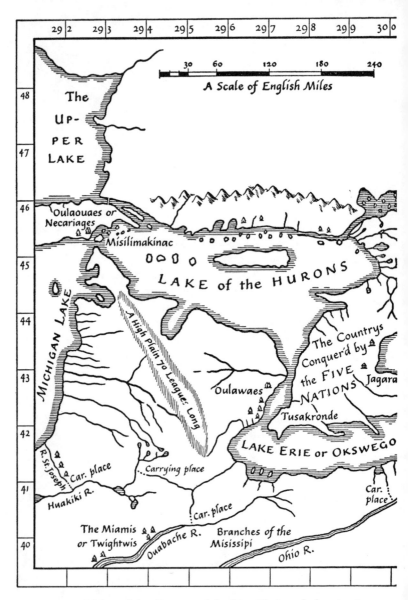

A Map of the Country of the Five Nations, belonging to
the Province of New York, and of the Lakes near which the

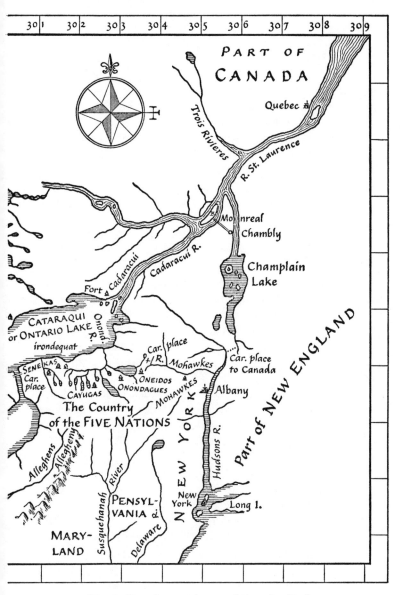

Nations of Far Indians live, with part of Canada. (Redrawn
from the map in the 1747 edition of Colden's *History*.)

Each Nation is an absolute Republick by its self, govern'd in all Publick Affairs of War and Peace by the Sachems or Old Men, whose Authority and Power is gain'd by and consists wholly in the Opinion the rest of the Nation have of their Wisdom and Integrity. They never execute their Resolutions by Compulsion or Force upon any of their People. Honour and Esteem are their Principal Rewards, as Shame & being Despised are their Punishments. They have certain Customs which they observe in their Publick Affairs with other Nations, and in their Private Affairs among themselves, which it is scandalous for any one not to observe, and draw after them publick or private Resentment when they are broke.

Their Generals and Captains obtain their Authority like-wise by the general Opinion of their Courage and Conduct, and loose it by a Failure in those Vertues.

Their Great Men, both Sachems and Captains, are generally poorer than the common People, for they affect to give away and distribute all the Presents or Plunder they get in their Treaties or War, so as to leave nothing to themselves. If they should once be suspected of Selfishness, they would grow mean in the opinion of their Country-men, and would consequently loose their Authority.

Their Affairs of Great Consequence, which concern all the Nations, are Transacted in a General Meeting of the Sachems of every Nation. These Conventions are generally held at Onnondaga, which is nearly in the Center of all the Five Nations. But they have fixed upon Albany to be the Place for their Solemn Treaties with the English Colonies.

The Tuscaroras, since the War they had with the People of Carolina, fled to the Five Nations, and are now incorporated with them, so that they now properly consist of Six Nations (tho' they still retain the old Name among the English.) The Tuscaroras, since they came under the Government of New-York, behave themselves well, and remain peaceable and quiet. By which may be seen the advantage of using the Indians well; and, I believe, if they were still better used, (as there is room enough to do it) the Indians would be proportionably more Useful to us.

As I am fond to think, that the present state of the Indian Nations exactly shows the most Ancient and Original Condition of almost every Nation; so I believe, here we may with more certainty see the Original Form of all Government, than in the most curious Speculations of the Learned; and that the Patriarchal, and other Schemes in Politicks are no better than Hypotheses in Philosophy, and as prejudicial to real Knowledge.

I shall only add the Character which Mons. De la Poterie gives of the Five Nations in his History of North-America, *viz.*

"When one talks (says he) of the Five Nations in France, they are thought, by a common Mistake, to be meer Barbarians, always thirsting after Human Blood; but their true Character is very different: They are the Fiercest and most Formidable People in North America, and at the same time as Politick and Judicious as well can be conceiv'd. This appears from their Management of the Affairs which they Transact, not only with the French and English, but likewise with almost all the Indian Nations of this vast Continent."

The Contents.

Part I.

From the first Knowledge the
Christians had of the Five Nations,
to the Time of the Happy Revolution
in Great Britain.

CHAP. I.

The Wars of the Five Nations with the Adirondacks and Quatoghies.

THE first Account we have of the Indians, who call themselves Rodinunchsiouni, now commonly known by the Name of the Five Nations, (and by the French call'd Les Iroquois) was from the French, who settled Canada under Mr. Champlain, their first Governor, in the year 1603. six years before the Dutch settled New-York. When the French first arrived, they found the Adirondacks (by the French called Algonkins) at War with the Five Nations, which, they tell us, was occasioned in the following manner.

(*a*) The Adirondacks formerly lived about one hundred Leagues above Trois Rivieres, where now the Utawawas live; at that time they imploy'd themselves wholly in Hunting, and the Five Nations made Planting of Corn their whole business, by which means they became useful to one another, and lived in Friendship together, the Five Nations exchanging with the Adirondacks Corn for Venison. The Adirondacks valued themselves, and their manner of living, as more Noble than that of the Five Nations, and despised them for that reason.

At last the Game began to be scarce with the Adirondacks, they therefore desired that some of the young Men of the Five Nations might joyn with them, and assist them in their

(*a*) Histoire de L'Amerique septentrionale par Mr. de Bacqueville de la Potherie, Vol. i. Lettre ii.

3

Hunting, which the Five Nations the more willingly agreed to, in hopes that thereby their People might acquire skill in Hunting.

It has been a constant Custom among all the Nations of Indians, to divide themselves into small Companies while they Hunt, and to divide likewise the Country among their several Parties, each having a space of 3 or four Miles Square alloted them, in which none of the others must pretend to Hunt; and if any Nation should encroach upon the Limits of another, in their hunting, they certainly draw a War upon themselves.

At this time the Adirondacks were obliged to spread them-themselves far, because of the scarcity of the Game, and each Party took some of the Five Nations along with them, who being less expert than the Adirondacks, perform'd most of the Drudgery in their March. One of these Parties, which consisted of six Adirondacks, and as many of the Five Nations, marched further than any of the rest, in hopes of the better Sport: They had, for a long time bad luck, so as to be obliged to live upon the Bark of Trees, and some Roots, which those of the Five Nations scraped out of the ground, from under the Snow. This extremity obliged the Adirondacks to part from those of the Five Nations, each making a seperate Company; and after they had agreed on a Day to return to a Cabbin where both of them left their Baggage, each took his Quarter to hunt in: The Adirondacks were unlucky, and return'd first to the Cabbin, where not finding those of the Five Nations, they did not doubt of their being dead of Hunger; but these young Men of the Five Nations were become dextrous with their Bows, and very cuning in approaching and surprizing their Game, which was chiefly owing to their being more patient and able to bear Fatigues and Hardships than the Adirondacks were, accordingly they soon arrived loaded with the flesh of Wild Cows. The Adirondacks could not believe that they were capable of such an Expedition, without being assisted by some of their Nation.

However, the Adirondacks received them with pleasant Countenances, and congratulated them on their Success. Those of the Five Nations made the other a Present of the best of their Venison: They eat together with much Civility, on both sides: But the Adirondacks becoming Jealous of this Success, conspired together, and in the Night time murdered all the six Men of the Five Nations, while they slept. Next Morning the Adirondacks follow'd their Foot-steps, by which they had return'd to the Cabbin, and found the place where they had hunted, and much Venison which they had killed, which the Adirondacks dryed, and carried home along with them.

The rest of the Five Nations enquired after their Companions; The Adirondacks answered very cooly, that they parted soon after they had left home, and they knew not what was become of them. But the People of the Five Nations being impatient to know something certain of their Companions, sent out several Parties in quest of them: They followed the Foot-steps of those Hunters, and found the six Dead Bodies, which the wild Beasts had dug up; and upon examination found they had been Murdered. They made many Complaints to the Chiefs of the Adirondacks, of the Inhumanity of this Murder, who contented themselves with blaming the Murderers, and ordering them to make some small Presents to the Relations of the murdered Persons, without being apprehensive of the Resentment of the Five Nations; for they look'd upon them as men not capable of taking any Revenge.

Those of the Five Nations smother'd their Anger, and not being willing to trust themselves any longer with the Adirondacks, they returned home to their own People, who then lived near Montreal on the Banks of St. Lawrence River. They gave an account of this Assassination to their Nation, who upon hearing it conceiv'd a vast Indignation against the Adirondacks, who being advised of the secret movements of the Five Nations, Resolv'd to oblige them to submit to their Law, by force of Arms. The Five Nations apprehending their Power, retired to the Southward of Cadarackui Lake, where they now live, and defended themselves at first but faintly against the Vigorous Attacks of the Adirondacks. But afterwards becoming more expert, and more used to War, they not only made a brave Defence, but likewise made themselves Masters of the great Lakes, and chased the Shawanons from thence.

While the two Nations were at War, the French arrived and settled in Canada, and the Five Nations having forced the Adirondacks to leave their own Country and retire towards Quebeck, the French thought themselves obliged to assist their New Allies, the Adirondacks, without examining into the Reasons of the War.

Thus began a War and Hatred between the French and the Five Nations, which cost the French much Blood, and more than once had like to have occasioned the entire Destruction of their Colony. The War had driven the Adirondacks to Quebec, and the desire of Trading with the French, had drawn likewise all their Allies that way, who agreed with them joyntly, to make War against the Five Nations, and to attack them in their own Country.

Mr. Champlain desiring to give his Allies Proof of his Love, and the Valour of the French Nation, put himself at the Head of a Body of Adirondacks, and passed with them into Corlars Lake, which from this time the French have called by Mr. Champlain's name.

They had not long been in the Lake before they discover'd a Body of the Five Nations going to War. As soon as they saw each other, Shouts and Crys began on both Sides. Mr. Champlain made his men keep their Canoes at some distance; The Five Nations in the mean time landed, and began to intrench themselves, by cutting down the Trees round them; The Adirondacks stopt their Canoes near the Enemy, & sent to offer them Battel, who answer'd, *That they must stay till Morning, when both sides would have the Advantage of the Day Light:* The night passed in Dancing and War Songs, mixed with a thousand Reproaches against each other. Mr.

Champlain had put some French in each Canoe, and order'd them not to show themselves, that their appearance might be the greater surprize to the Enemy, in the time of the Battel. As soon as day light appeared, the Adirondacks landed, in order of Battel, & the Five Nations to the Number of 200 Men marched out of their Intrenchments, and put themselves in order, with three Captains in the Front, having large Plumes of Feathers on their Heads, and then advanced with a grave Air and slow Pace. The Adirondacks gave a great Shout and open'd to the Right and Left, to give room for Mr. Champlain and the French to advance: This new Sight surprized the Enemy, and made them halt, to consider it, upon which the French firing, the three Captains were killed: This more surpriz'd the Five Nations; for they knew that their Captains had a kind of Cuirass made of pieces of Wood join'd together, that was Proof against Arrows, and they could not perceive in what manner the Wound was given, by which they fell so suddenly. Then the Adirondacks gave a terrible Shout, and attacked the Enemy, who received them bravely, but a second Volley from the French, put them into such Confusion (having never before seen fire Arms) that they immediately fled. The Adirondacks took twelve Prisoners, and as the Custom of the Indians is, burnt one of them alive, with great Cruelty; His Torment had continued much longer than it did, if Mr. Champlain had not in Compassion & abhorrence of such Barbarity, Shot the poor Wretch thro' the Head.

The Adirondacks having their Numbers thus very much encreased, and their fire Arms giving them new Confidence, proposed nothing less to themselves, than the entire Destruction of the Five Nations, by open Force; And upon this their Young Warriors became Fierce and Insolent, and could not be kept under any Discipline, Order or Subjection to their Chiefs or Captains, but upon all Occasions rashly attacked the Enemy, who were oblig'd to keep themselves upon the Defensive, and to make up what they wanted in Force, by Stratagems, and a skillful management of the War. The Young Men of the Five Nations soon perceived the Advantages they gain'd by this Conduct, and every day grew more submissive to their Captains, and diligent in executing any Enterprize, while the Adirondacks confiding in their Numbers and their fire Arms, thought of nothing but of Conquering by meer Force.

The Five Nations sent out small Parties only, who meeting with great Numbers of the Adirondacks, retired before them, with seeming Fear and Terror, while the Adirondacks pursued them with Fury, and without thought, till they were cunningly drawn into Ambuscades, where most of their men were kill'd or taken Prisoners, with little or no loss to the Five Nations.

By these means and their being frequently surprized by the Five Nations, while they remain'd confident in their Number, the Adirondacks wasted away, and their boldest Soldiers were almost entirely destroyed, while the Number of the Five Nations rather encreased by the addition of the Prisoners which they took from the Shawanons.

It has been a constant Maxim with the Five Nations, to save the Children and Young Men of the People they Conquer, to adopt them into their own Nation, and to educate them as their own Children, without Distinction; These young People soon forget their own Country and Nation; and by this Policy the Five Nations make up the Losses which their Nation suffers by the People they loose in War. The wisest and best Soldiers of the Adirondacks when it was too late, discovered that they must imitate and learn the Art of War from those Enemies, that they at first Despised. Now five of their Chief Captains endeavour to perform by themselves singly, with Art and by Stratagem, what they could not perform by Force at the Head of their Armies; but they having no longer any hopes of Conquering their Enemies, their thoughts were only set on Revenge.

The Five Nations had taken one of the chief Captains of the Adirondacks, and had burnt him alive. This gave Piskaret, who was the chief Captain of the Adirondacks so deep a Resentment, that the Difficulty or Danger of the most desperate Attempt made no Impression upon his Spirit, where he had the hope of Revenge.

I shall give the Particulars of this from the French Accounts; for by it the nature of the Indians, and the manner of their making War, may be more easily understood.

Piskaret, with four other Captains, set out from Trois Rivieres in one Canoe, each being provided with three Fuzees. In two Days they reach'd Sorel River, where they perceiv'd five Canoes of the Five Nations with ten Men in each. At first those of the Five Nations believed that this Canoe was the van of some considerable Party, and therefore went from it with all the force of their Paddles. When they saw that after a considerable time, no others followed, they returned, and as soon as they came within call, they raised their War-Shout, which they call Sassakue, and bid Piskaret and his Fellows Surrender. He answered, That he was their Prisoner, and that he could no longer survive the Captain they had burnt; but that he might not be accused of surrendering Cowardly, he bid them advance to the middle of the River which they did, with surprizing Swiftness. Piskaret had before hand loaded all his Arms with two Bullets each, which he joyn'd together with a small Wire ten Inches in length with design to tear the Canoes in pieces (which it could not fail to do, they being made only of Birch Bark) and gave his Companions Direction, each to chuse a Canoe, and level his shot between Wind and Water.

As the Canoes approached, he made as if he had design'd to escape; and to prevent him, those of the Five Nations seperated from each other with too much Precipitation, and Surrounded him. The Adirondacks, the better to amuse the Enemy, sung their Death Song, as ready to surrender themselves, when every one suddenly took his Piece and fired upon the Canoes, which they Reiterated three times, with the Arms that lay ready. Those of the Five Nations were extreamly surpriz'd; for Fire

Arms were still terrible to them, and they tumbled out of their Canoes, which immediately sunk. The Adirondacks knock't them all on the head in the Water, except some of the chiefs that they made Prisoners, who's Fate was as cruel as that of the Adirondack Captain, who had been burnt alive.

Piskaret was so far from having his Revenge glutted with this Slaughter, and the cruel Torments with which he made his Prisoners dye, that it seem'd rather to give a keener edge to it; for he soon after attempted another enterprize in which the boldest of his Country-men durst not accompany him.

He was well acquainted with the Country of the Five Nations, he set out alone about the time that the Snow began to melt, with the precaution of putting the hinder part of his Snow Shoes forward, that if any should happen upon his foot-steps, they might think that he was gone the contrary way; and for further security went along a Ridge, where the Snow was melted, and where his foot-steps could not be discovered, but in a few places. When he found himself near one of the Villages of the Five Nations he hid himself in a hollow Tree: In the Night he found out a Place nearer at hand, and more proper to retire into, for the execution of any Enterprize. He found four Piles of Wood standing close together, which the Indians had provided against the Winter and their busie times, in the middle of which was a hollow place, in which he thought he could safely hide. The whole Village was fast asleep when he enter'd a Cabbin, kill'd four Persons and took off their Scalps, being all that were in the House, and then re-turn'd quietly into his Hole. In the Morning the whole Village was in an Alarm, as soon as the Murder was discovered, and the young Men made all possible haste to follow the Murderer. They discover'd Piskarets foot-steps, which ap-pear'd to them to be the foot-steps of some Person that fled; this encourag'd them in their Pursuit: Sometimes they lost the Tract, and sometimes found it again, till at last they entirely lost it, where the Snow was melted, and they were forced to return, after much useless fatigue. Piskaret quiet in the midst of his Enemies waited with impatience for the Night. As soon as he saw that it was time to act (*viz.* in the first part of the night, when the Indians are observed to sleep very fast) he enter'd into another Cabbin, where he kill'd every Person in it, & immediately retir'd into his Wood-pile. In the morning there was a greater Outcry than before, nothing was seen but Wailing, Tears, and a general Consternation. Every one runs in quest of the Murderer, but no Tract to be seen besides the Tract which they saw the day before. They search'd the Woods, Swamps and Clifts of the Rocks, but no Murderer to be found. They began to suspect Piskaret, who's Boldness and Cunning was too well known to them. They agreed that two men next night should watch in every Cabbin. All day long he was contriving some new Stratagem, he bundles up his Scalps, and in the night he slips out of his lurking place, He approaches one of the Cabbins as quietly as possible and peeps thro' a hole to see what could be done, there he perceived Guards on the Watch, he went to another, where he found the same care. When he discover'd that they were everywhere upon their Guard he resolved to strike his last blow, and opened a Door, where he found a Centinel nodding with his Pipe in his mouth, Piskaret split his Scull with his Hatchet, but had not time to take his Scalp, for another man who watched at the other end of the Cabbin, raised the cry, and Piskaret fled. The whole Village immediately was in an Uproar, while he got off as fast as he could; Many pursued him, but as he was so swift as to run down the Wild Cows and the Deer, the pursuit gave him no great uneasiness; When he perceived they came near him, he would Halloe to them, to quicken their pace, then spring from them like a Buck. When he gain'd any distance he would loiter till they came near, then halloe, and fly. Thus he continued all day, with design to tire them out, with the hopes of over-taking him.

As they pursued only a single Man, five or six only of the Nimblest young Men continued the Chace, till being tired they were forced to rest in the Night, which when Piskaret observed, he hid himself near them in a hollow Tree. They had not time to take Victuals with them, and being wearied & hungry, and not apprehending any Attack from a single Person that fled, they all soon fell a sleep. Piskaret observ'd them, fell upon them, kill'd them all, and carried away their (*b*) Scalps.

These Stories may seem incredible to many, but will not appear to be Improbable to those who know how extreamly Revengeful the Indians naturally are. That they every day undertake the greatest Fatigues, the longest Journeys, and the greatest Dangers, to gratifie that Devouring Passion, which seems to gnaw their Souls, and gives them no ease till it is satisfied. All Barbarous Nations have been observed to be Revengful and Cruel, the certain Consequences of an un-bounded Revenge, as the Curbing of these Passions is the happy Effect of being Civilized.

The Five Nations are so much delighted with Stratagems in War, that no Superiority of their Force makes them neglect them. They amused therefore the Adirondacks and their Allies, the Quatoghies, (called by the French, Hurons) by sending to the French, and desiring Peace. The French desired them to receive some Priests among them, in hopes that these pru-dent Fathers would by some Art reconcile them to the French, and engage their Affections. The Five Nations ac-cepted the Offer, and some Jesuits went along with them. But after they had the Jesuits in their Power, they used them only as Hostages, and by that means obliged the French to be Neuter, while they prepared to Attack the Adirondacks and Quatoghies, and accordingly entirely destroy'd the Quatoghies in a Battel fought within two Leagues of Quebeck, while the French durst not give their Allies any assistance.

Indeed the French Author says, That if the Five Nations

(*b*) These are the Trophies of Victory which all the Indian Nations carry home with them, if they have time to flea the Scalp from the Skull of their Enemies, when they have killed them; and sometimes they are so cruel as to flea the Scalp off, without killing them, or otherwise wounding them, but leave them in this miserable Condition with their Skull bare.

had known the weakness of the French at that time, they might easily have destroyed that Colony.

The Defeat of the Quatoghies struck Terror into all the Allies of the Adirondacks, who were at that time very Numerous, because of the benefit of the French Trade, which they had by their means; for before that time the Indians had not any Iron Tool among them.

The Nepiceriniens, who then lived on the Banks of St. Laurence River, fled to the Northward, in hopes that the extream Coldness of the Climate, and a barren Soil, would free them from the fear they had of the Five Nations. The remainder of the Quatoghies fled with the Utawawas Southwestward, and for their greater Security settled in an Island, which the French still call by their Name, which being further than the Name of the Five Nations had at that time reached, they thought themselves secure by the Distance of the Place.

This Expedition having succeeded so well, the Five Nations gave out, that they intended next Winter to visit Yonnondio (the name they give to the Governor of Canada.) These visits are always made with much Show. They gather'd together 1000 or 1200 Men, and passing over Corlaers Lake, they fell in with Nicolet River, where it falls into the South side of Lake St. Pierre, in St. Laurence River, eight Leagues above Trois Rivieres; Six Scouts marched three Leagues before the Army, who met with Piskaret, as he return'd from Hunting, loaded with the Tongues of wild Cows. As they came near him, they sang their Song of Peace, and Piskaret taking them for Ambassadors, stopt, and sung his. It is probable that he having glutted his private Revenge, and his Nation having been long harassed with a Cruel War, he too greedily swallow'd the Bait: Peace being what he and all his Nation earnestly desir'd. He invited them therefore to go along with him to his Village, which was but two or three Leagues further: and as he went, he told them, that the Adirondacks were divided into two Bodies, one of which hunted on the North side of St. Laurence River at Wabmache, three Leagues above Trois Rivieres, and the other at Nicolet. One of the Scouts had on purpose staid behind, this Man followed Piskaret, and coming up behind him, knockt him on the Head with his Hatchet. Then they all returned to their Army with Piskaret's Head. The Five Nations immediately divided likewise into two Bodies, they surprized the Adirondacks, and cut them in pieces.

Thus the most War-like and Polite Nation of all the Indians in North-America was almost entirely Destroy'd by a People they at first despised, and by a War which their Pride and Injustice brought upon them. Immorality has ever ruin'd the Nations where it abounded, whether they were Civilized or Barbarians, as Justice and strict Discipline has made others Flourish and grow Powerful.

A very few Adirondacks now remain in some Villages near Quebeck, who still waste away and decay, by their drinking Strong Waters, tho' when the French first settled Quebeck, 1500 Men of them lived between that and Silleri, which are only a League distant, besides those that lived at Saguenay, Trois Rivieres, and some other places. After this Battle the Adirondacks have never been considered as of any consequence, either in Peace or War.

The Quatoghies and Utawawas soon began to be in want of the European Commodities, and their desire to make themselves considerable among their new Friends, set them upon attempting to return to trade at Quebeck, by which means the place of their retreat was discovered to the Five Nations, who not having their Revenge satiated, so long as any of that Nation remain'd, resolved at all hazards to march through these vast unknown Deserts, to satisfy their cruel Passion. The Quatoghies had the good Fortune to discover them time enough to make their Escape, and fled to the Putewatemies, who liv'd a days Journey further, where they and all the Neighbouring Nations secur'd themselves in a large Fort. The Five Nations followed, but being in want of Provisions, they could not attempt a Siege, and therefore propos'd a Treaty to the Putewatemies, which was accepted. The Putewatemies agreed to a League of Friendship, in which they acknowledged the Five Nations to be the Master of all the Nations round them, applauded their Valour, and promised to supply them with Provisions, but would not trust themselves out of their Fort. The Putewatemies accordingly sent them out a supply of Provisions, but with design to effect, by Treachery, what they durst not attempt by Force; for they Poison'd all the Provisions. This was discover'd to them by an old Quatoghie, who had a Son Prisoner among the Five Nations. His affection for his Son overcame his hatred to his Country's Enemies. This Treachery enraged the Five Nations against the Pute-watemies, and the Neighbouring Nations, but Famine obliged them to return at this time, and to seperate their Army into Parties, the better to provide for their Subsistence by Hunt-ing. One of these Parties fell in with a Village of the Chich-taghicks (call'd by the French, Ilinois) and surpriz'd the old Men, Women and Children, when the young Men were abroad Hunting, but they upon their return gather'd all the rest of the Villages, pursued the party of the Five Nations, and re-cover'd the Prisoners.

This was the first time that the Five Nations had appear'd in those Parts, but their Name was become so Terrible, that the Chicktaghicks, notwithstanding of this Advantage, left their Country, and fled to the Nations that lived Westward, till the general Peace was settled by the French, and then they return'd to their own Country.

CHAP. II.

Their Wars and Treaties of Peace with the French, from 1665. to 1683. and their Affairs with New-York in that Time.

IN June, 1665, Mons. de Trasi being Appointed Vice-Roy of America, arrived at Quebeck, after he had visited all the Islands in the West-Indies, and brought with him four Com-

panies of Foot. In September of the same year Mr. Coursel
arrived with the Commission of Governor General of Canada,
with eleven Vessels, which transported a Regiment, and several
Families, with all things necessary for the establishing of a
Colony. The French Force being thus so considerably aug-
mented, he resolved in the Winter to send out a Party against
the Mohawks, which by the Cold, and their not knowing the
use of Snow-Shoes, suffered very much, without doing any
thing against the Enemy.

This Party fell in with Schenectady, a small Town which
Corlaer (a considerable Man among the Dutch) had then
newly settled. When they appear'd near Schenectady they
were almost kill'd with Cold and Hunger, and the Indians,
who then were in that Village, had entirely finished their
Ruin, if Corlaer, (in Compassion of fellow Christians) had
not contriv'd their escape. He had a mighty Influence over the
Indians, and it is from him that all the Governors of New-
York are call'd Corlaer by the Indians to this Day, tho' he
himself never was Governor. He perswaded the Indians that
this was but a small Party of the French Army, come to amuse
them, that the great Body was gone directly towards their
Castles, and that it was necessary for them immediately to go
in Defence of their Wives and Children: which they did. As
soon as the Indians were gone, he sent to the French, and
supply'd them with Provisions to carry them back. The French
Governor, in order to Reward so signal a Service, invited
Corlaer to Canada, and, no doubt, with design to make use
of his Interest with the Indians in some Project, in favour of
the French Colony; but as he went through the Lake (by the
French call'd Champlain) his Canoe was Overset, and he
drowned. From this Accident that Lake has ever since been
call'd Corlaers Lake by the People of New-York.

There is a Rock in this Lake, on which the Waves dash and
fly up to a very great height, when the Wind blows strong; the
Indians fancy, that an Old Indian lives under this Rock, who
has the Power of the Winds, and therefore as they pass this

Rock in their Voyages through this Lake, they always throw a Pipe or some Tobacco, or something else to this Old Indian, and pray a favourable Wind. The English that often pass with them, sometimes laugh at them; but they are sure to be told of Corlaers Death with a grave air. *Your great Country-man Corlaer* (say they) *as he passed by this Rock, jested at our Fathers making Presents to this Old Indian, and in derision turn'd up his Back-side towards the Rock, but this Affront cost him his Life.*

The next Spring the Vice-Roy and the Governor, with 28 Companies of Foot, and all the Inhabitants of the Colony, marched into the Country of the Mohawks, with a design to destroy this Nation, which by the War not only prevented their Commerce with other Indians, but even prevented the Settlement of the Colony. This certainly was a bold Attempt, to march thus above 250 Leagues from Quebeck, through unknown Forrests; but all they were able to do, was to burn some of their Villages, and to Murder some Old Men, that (like the Old Roman Senators) would rather dye than desert their Houses.

This Expedition, however, gave the Five Nations Apprehensions they had not before; for they never before that saw so great a Number of Europeans, whose Fire-Arms were extreamly Terrible, and they therefore thought proper to send and beg a Peace, which was concluded in 1667.

But they being naturally very Enterprizing and Haughty, a Party of the Five Nations met with a Party of the French a hunting, and quarrelled with them. The French Author does not inform us of the particulars: But it seems the Indians had the Advantage, for they kill'd several of the French and carried one Prisoner into their own Country. Mons. De Coursel sent to Threaten the Five Nations with War, if they did not deliver up these Murderers.

The Five Nations being at this time apprehensive of the French Power, sent Agariata, the Captain of the Company that did the Mischief, with forty others, to beg Peace; but

Mr. Coursel was resolved to make an Example of Agariata. He therefore ordered him to be Hang'd, in the Presence of his Country-men, which kind of Death they having never seen before, it struck them with Terror, & the French, think that this Severity was a great means of preserving the Peace till the year 1683.

The Dutch having settled New-York in 1609. (which they call'd the New-Netherlands) they enter'd into an Alliance with the Five Nations, which continued without any Breach on either side, and were frequently useful to the French, in saving the French that were Prisoners from the Cruelty of the Indians, as before observed.

In 1664. New-York was taken by the English, who immediately entred into an Alliance and Friendship with the Five Nations, which has continued without the least Breach to this Day. History, I am afraid, cannot inform us of an Instance of the Most Christian or Most Catholick King Observing a League so strictly, and for so long a time as these Barbarians have done.

Both the English and French (Peace being every where settled) endeavour to extend their Commerce and Alliances among the Indians which lie to the Westward of New-York. The French in their Measures discover'd a Design of Conquering and Commanding; for Mr. de Frontenac, who had succeeded in the Government of Canada in the Year 1672, perswaded the Indians to allow him to build a Fort at Cadarackui, under the Notion of a Store for Merchandize and security for his Traders, and under the same pretence built small Forts at some other considerable Passes far in the Country.

The English and Dutch Prosecuted their Measures only with the Arts of Peace, by sending People among the Indians to gain their Affections, and to perswade them to come to Albany to Trade; but ev'n these honest Designs met with Obstruction, and had not so considerable Success, by reason of the War with the Dutch, as otherwise they might have had; for in the Year 1674. New-York being Surpriz'd by the Dutch, and Restor'd, the alterations in Government and of Masters, ob-

structed very much the designs of gaining the Indians. Their
Trade was likewise considerably hindred by the War, which
the Five Nations had with the (c) River Indians, which forced
many of the River Indians to seek shelter among the Utawawas, who fell under the French Government.

At last the English, Dutch and French having made Peace
in Europe, and the Governor of New-York likewise having
obtain'd a Peace between the Five Nations and Mahikanders
or River Indians, the English and French were at full liberty to
prosecute their designs of extending their Commerce among
the Indians, which both did with very considerable success and
advantage to the Inhabitants of their Colonies.

But this Justice must be done to the French, that they far
exceeded the English in the daring attempts of some of their
Inhabitants, in travelling very far among unknown Indians,
discovering new Countries, and every where spreading the
Fame of the French Name and Grandeur, by making themselves the Arbitrators in all difference between the Indian Nations. The Sieur Perot deserves to be remember'd, who pushed
his Discoveries as far as the Putewatemies and Indians living
round the farther Lakes, with the greatest Fatigues and Danger. He acquired the Languages of many Nations, and brought
them to Canada to Trade, before the Peace was made with
the Five Nations. In the Year 1667 he accompanied the
Officer that was sent to the Fall of St. Mary, to take Possession
of all that Country, in the name of the French King, in the
presence of many of the Sachems of the Nations that liv'd
round the Lakes, where there was an Alliance agree'd to with
the French, but (ev'n by the French Books) no Subjection
was Promised.

In the Year 1697. Mr. De la Sale built a Sloop or Bark of
sixty Tons on Ohswego Lake, and provided her with great
Guns. He carried this Vessel as far as Missilimackinack, and
there loaded her with Furrs and Skins, and then went on the
Discovery of the Misissipi. He only left five or six French on

(c) The Indians living on the Banks of Hudsons River within or near the
English Settlements.

board to carry her back to Oniagara: But the Indians entertain'd such a Jealousy of this floating Castle, that they resolv'd
secretly to destroy it, tho' they exprest nothing to Mr. De la
Sale, but Admiration of the extraordinary Machine, and sent
for all the Nations round to come to see it. When they were
together they consulted how to surprize and destroy it; and
this design they kept so secret, not only before the Execution,
that Mr. De la Sale had no suspicion of it, but afterwards
likewise, for it was long before it was known what became of
this Vessel. At first they thought of killing all the French
among them, and throwing themselves on the English for their
Protection; but their Courage fail'd them. They thought they
might act with more security after Mr. De la Sale and his
Company should be gone on their intended Discoveries. The
French having no suspicion of their designs, permitted a
Number of Indians to come on board in a Bay where the
Bark came to an Anchor, in her return, and the Indians taking
advantage of their Numbers, and the security of the French,
murder'd the Men and burnt the Vessel.

The Courage and Resolution of these Gentlemen ought to
be taken Notice of, for their Honour, notwithstanding that
the English say, that the Barrenness and Poverty of Canada
pushes the Men of Spirit there upon Enterprizes they would
not attempt if they liv'd in the Province of New-York.

CHAP. III.

*The Affairs of the Five Nations with the Neigh-
bouring English Colonies.*

THE Five Nations being now amply supply'd with Fire-Arms
and Ammunition, give full swing to their War-like Genius,
and therefore resolv'd to Revenge the Affronts they had at any

time receiv'd from their Neighbours. The nearest Nations as they were attackt, commonly flying to those that were further off, the Five Nations pursued. This, together with a desire they had of Conquering and of making all the Nations round them their Tributaries, or to acknowledge the Five Nations to be their Masters, made the Five Nations over-run the greatest part of North-America. They carried their Arms as far South as Carolina, and to the Northward of New-England, and as far West as the River Misissipi, over a vast Country which extends 1200 Miles in Length, from North to South, and about six hundred Miles in Breadth, and entirely Destroyed many Nations that made Resistance.

These War-like Expeditions often prov'd Troublesom to the Colonies of Virginia and Maryland; for not only the Indians who were Friends to those Colonies, became Victims to the Fury of the Five Nations, but the Christian Inhabitants likewise were involv'd often in the same Calamity.

For this reason about the year 1677. the Government of Maryland sent Coll. Coursey to Albany to make a League of Friendship between Virginia and Maryland on the one part, and the Five Nations on the other; but this League was soon shaken by some Parties of the Oneydoes, Onondagas and Sennekas, who were out when this Covenant was made, and were ignorant of it. One of these Parties met with the Susquehana Indians, who were in Friendship with Maryland, and fell upon them, kill'd four, and took six Prisoners. Five of these Prisoners fell to the share of the Sennekas, who, as soon as they arriv'd in their Country, sent them back with Presents, to shew that they kept to their League with Maryland; but the Oneydoes detain'd the Prisoner they had.

Another Party that went against the Canagesse Indians (Friends of Virginia) were surprized by a Troop of Virginia Horse, who kill'd one Man and took a Woman Prisoner. The Indians in Revenge kill'd four of the Inhabitants, and carried away their Scalps, with six Christian Prisoners.

The Mohawks all this while kept themselves strictly to

their League, and suffered none of their Indians to go towards
Virginia and Maryland.

There is reason to think that the Dutch, who lived at
Schenectady at that time, spirited up the Indians against the
English; For the Commander at Albany hearing that the Five
Nations, (the Oneydoes especially) were in an Alarm from
some Jealousy that they had entertain'd of the English at
New-York sent Arnout and Daniel, two Interpreters of the
Indian Language, to perswade them to come to Albany, in
order to be assured of the English Friendship, and to have
their Jealousy remov'd. Which the Interpreters having happily
brought to pass, Swerisse, one of the chief Men or Sachims
of the Oneydoes excus'd his Country-men at Albany, the 15th
of February 1678,9. as follows,

"Father Corlaer;

"We are now come to speak to you of some strange Oc-
curences that have lately happened.

"Last Harvest one of our Indians, call'd, Treuhtanendo,
went to Schenectady to buy goods; he was told of the Mischief we had done in Virginia; To which the People of
Schenectady added, That the English of this Government were
very Angry, and that they would kill us.

"Soon afterwards another of our Indians, call'd, Adagounwa,
went to Schenectady, in his way to Albany; He was told by
the People there, That if he went forward to Albany he
might sing to Morrow, for the English there would bind and
kill him; Whereupon he and another Indian immediately
returned, and brought this Report to our Castle at Oneido.

"But we now see the Governors good heart, notwithstanding
of all this bad News.

"At last the People of Schenectady told five of our Indians,
who intended for Albany, That if they went forward they
would all be Dead Men; upon which one run immediately
back, but the other four went forward. This Man, (who is
called Ounwahrarihta) told us, That the other four Men

were taken by the English, and that two or three hundred Men were upon their way to fight us. Upon hearing of this, I acknowledge, that though I, Swerisse, be a Sachem, I left the Affair wholly to our Soldiers, seeing that they were Soldiers who came against us; Whereupon our Men immediately Resolv'd to Fortifie the Castle.

"While this was doing the War-Shout was raised. Our Men call'd out, *That Horse-men came against us; Now we shall be put to it.* These prov'd to be the two Interpreters, who being receiv'd into the Castle, our young Soldiers, whose Spirits had been vehemently raised, run round them with their Hatchets in their hands, threatning to kill them. But I, Swerisse, did what I could to pacifie our Men, and told the Messengers, *That we would hear them to Morrow.*

"Father Corlaer; We desire that your Anger may be appeased, and that your Mind may be quieted. We give no credit to the stories which our Indians brought us from Schenectady, and we shall not believe any such Stories for the future Seeing all of us to the Westward, ev'n from New-York to the Sennekas, are under one Government, Why is Schenectady the only bad place? for We hold firmly to the Old Covenant."

Then he gave a Belt of Wampum (*d*).

He in the next place gave an account of what had happened in Virginia, And then said,

"Father Corlaer;

"Have Pity on our Indian Prisoners, as We have had on

(*d*) Wampum is the current Money among the Indians, it is made of the large Whelk Shell (*Briccinum*) and shaped like long Beads. With this, put upon strings, they make these Belts, which they give in all their Treaties, as signs of Confirmation, to remain with the other Party. The Wampum is of two sorts, *viz.* White and Black; the Black is the rarest, and most valuable. By a regular mixing of the Black and White they distinguish their Belts with various Figures, which they often suit to the Occasion of making use of them. Wampum is called Zewant by the Dutch in this Province.

these Prisoners (viz. *A Woman and her two Children*) which we now deliver to you, notwithstanding that they have been giv'n away, according to our Custom. We pray therefore his Honour to take Pity on our People that are Prisoners, especially on the Indian Woman, his Kins-Woman, whom he hath adopted as a Grand-Child. Let them be Released, if alive, otherwise give us some of the Canastoga Indians in their room. As to the other three Christian Prisoners, the Woman and her two Children that are yet with us, We desire first to have our Indians Restored, or others in their room, before they be Delivered."

Governor Andross, being acquainted by Letter with this last Proposal of the Oneydoes, required the immediate Delivery of the Christian Prisoners, and promised to write to Virginia to have the Indian Prisoners saved. Some presents being given to the Oneydoes, they answered,

"We Thank the Governor for his good Inclination and Affection. Our Heart is good, and we see his Heart is likewise good; if it were otherwise we could not live: We thank the Governor for the Present now giv'n us: It is his wellcome from England.

"Father Corlaer, We are your Children, and the Mohawks, your Brethren, are likewise our Fathers. We rejoyce because your Hearts are good. Since the Governor is not satisfied with these three Prisoners, we have now unanimously Resolved to bring the other three which are still with us, as soon as possible; but the Rivers are now so full of Water, that we cannot bring them this Moon, but the next Moon, I, Swerisse, promise to come with them.

"We obey the Governor's Orders, that we may not be ashamed, and therefore We Release all the Prisoners. We hope the Governor will likewise act so as he need not be ashamed.

"We do not now say, that we will see our Prisoners before we deliver the other Christians, but refer this Affair wholly to the Governor's Wisdom, which, we hope, will tend to our good and continued Wellfair. And say again, That we will bring the three Christian Prisoners by the first opportunity of fair Weather.

"We likewise make known to our Father Corlaer, That in our Fury and Anger (after the People of the South had fallen upon us) We took these six Prisoners, and afterwards four Scalps were brought by our People, and no more.

"We speak as Oneydoes, for our selves. If the Susquehana or Delaware Indians have done any Mischief, let not that be imputed to us.

"Eight of our People are now out against the Christians, of which we told Aernout and Daniel when they were at our Castle. They know nothing of what we have now agree'd to, and therefore if they should happen to do any harm, let it be passed by, for they are entirely Ignorant of the Governor's Orders. If they shall do any thing, we shall not keep it secret. If any of the Christian Prisoners shall dye before we bring them, we should be sorry; yet they are Mortal."

Accordingly in May following the Oneydoes brought the other three Prisoners to Albany. And on the 24th of that Month Swerisse made the following Speech, when he deliver'd them to the Commander at Albany, and the Commissioners for Indian Affairs.

"Bretheren;

"We are come to this place with much Trouble, as we did last Winter, and renew the Request we then made, that six Indians be delivered to us in the room of the six Christians, in case those of our People who are Prisoners in Virginia be dead. None of our Indians have gone out against the English since we were last here; but we have told you that some of ours were then out, who were ignorant of the Governor's Orders, and we desired that if they happen'd to do any harm, it might not be ill taken. Now thirteen of our People who went against our Indian Enemies, met with eighteen English on Horseback, as far from any of the English Plantations as Cahnuaga (*e*) is from Albany. They fir'd upon our People; ours being Soldiers, return'd their Fire and kill'd two Men and two Horses, and brought away their Scalps.

"It would be convenient that the Governor acquaint the People of Virginia, not to send their Men so far abroad, for if they should happen to meet our Parties in their way against our Enemies, the Cahnowas, whom the English call Arogisti, dangerous Consequences might follow.

"We have now submitted to the Governor's Order, in bringing the three other Christian Prisoners. When we were here last Winter, we left the Affair of our Prisoners wholy to the Governor, and promised to bring the three Christian Prisoners that remain'd with us. This we have now perform'd: But where are our Prisoners, or if they be dead, the others in their room, tho' it be already so late in the Spring: However, we still refer this to the Governor.

(Then taking the Christian Girl, who was a Prisoner, by the hand, said) "This Girl was deliver'd to an Indian Squa (*f*) here present, who's Brother then was kill'd. If we had been full of Wrath, and not afraid of further Inconveniencies, we would have burnt her.

(Taking the Boy, another of the three, by the hand, said) "This Boy was giv'n to an Indian here present, but he is now free. We have now perform'd our Promises, and are not ashamed. We hope Corlaer, who Governs the whole Country, will likewise do that of which he needeth not be ashamed.

"Corlaer governs the whole Land, from New-York to Albany, and from thence to the Sennekas Land; We who are his Subjects shall faithfully keep the Covenant Chain: Let him perform his Promise, as we have perform'd ours, that the Covenant Chain be not broken on his side, who governs the whole Country.

"Corlaers Limits, as we have said, stretch so far ev'n to Jacob my Friend, or Jacob Young, and we have heard that

(*e*) The first Mohawk Castle.
(*f*) A Woman.

Corlaer is in good Correspondence with Virginia and Maryland; Why is it then that our People, who are Prisoners, are not restored? Let what we now say be well observed, for we have observed the Governor's Orders.

Lastly (taking the Woman Prisoner by the hand, said) "This Woman was given to that Indian, (*pointing,*) but is now free, being the sixth. If those of our People who are Prisoners be Dead, let us have six Indians in their room. It is not by my Authority that these Prisoners have been released, but by the good Will of them to whom they were given.

"Our Soldiers are to go out against the Dewagunhas, let us have Ammunition cheap."

Then the Commissioners gave them Presents for their kind Usage of the Prisoners.

After which Swerisse stood up and said, "Let Corlaer take care that the Indian Squa that is wanting come again, and for those that are killed, others in their room. If Corlaer will not hearken to us in this Affair, we shall not hereafter hearken to him in any."

They hearing afterwards that these last words were ill taken, Swerisse, Jehonongera and Kanohguage, three of the chief Oneydo Sachems excused it, saying, "What we said of not hearkening any more to Corlaer, was not from the heart, but only by way of Discourse, to make Corlaer more careful to release our People that are Prisoners; for it was said after your Answer, and without laying down either Bever or any Belt or Wampum, as we always do when we make (g) Propositions; Therefore we desire that if it be noted, it may be blotted out, and not made known to Corlaer; for we hold firmly to our Covenant, as we said in our Propositions."

They at the same time told, That the Sinnondowans (h)

(g) The word Proposition has been always used by the Commissioners for Indian Affairs at Albany, to signifie Proposals or Articles, in the Treaties or Agreements made with the Indians.

(h) A Castle of the Sennekas, from whence the French call all the Sennekas, Tsonontouan.

came to them with eight Belts, desiring that they should no longer prosecute the War with Virginia, or Virginia Indians, but to go with them to War against the Dowaganhas, (*i*) a Nation lying to the North-west ward; and that the Sennekas did desire them to set these Christians at Liberty, and to carry them to Albany. All which they said they promised to do.

The Five Nations continuing still to be troublesome to Virginia, that Government, in September following, sent Col. William Kendall and Col. Southley Littleton to Albany, to Renew and Confirm the League between Virginia and the Five Nations. Col. Littleton dy'd at Albany before the Indians arriv'd. Col. Kendall spoke to the Oneydoes, as follows,

The Propositions of Col. William Kendall and Col. Southley Littleton Commissioners sent by the Governor, Council and Burgesses of Virginia, at a Grand Assembly held in James-City.

"We are come from Virginia, being, as all these Countries are, under the Great King Charles, to speak to you upon Occasion of some of yours having entred our Houses, taken away and destroy'd our Goods and People, and brought some of our Women and Children Captives into your Castles, contrary to your Faith and Promise. It is also a Breach of the Peace made with Col. Coursey, without any Provocation or Injury in the least done by us, or disturbing you in your Hunting, Trade, or Passing, until you were found taking our Corn out of our Fields, and plundering and burning our Houses.

"Tho' your Actions already done are sufficient Reasons to enduce us to a violent War against you, which might engage all our Confederate English Neighbours, Subjects to our great King Charles; yet through the great Respect we have to and the Perswasions of the Governor here, whom we find your great Friend, and the Information that he has given us, that you have quietly and peaceably deliver'd to him the

(*i*) Comprehended under the General name of Utawawas.

Prisoners you had taken from us, who are also returned safely into our Country, and your Excusing the same, and Inclination to continue Peaceable, without Injuring us for the future, We are therefore willing, and have, and do forgive all the Damages which you have done our People, tho' very great, Provided neither you nor any living among you, for the future, do not offend or molest our People or Indians living amongst us.

"And we do acquaint you, that we have a Law in our Country, that all Indians coming near Christians must stand still, and lay down their Arms, as a token of their being Friends, or otherwise are taken and lookt upon or destroyed as Enemies. Therefore desire you will take notice thereof accordingly, for we have many of our People in the Woods abroad every way."

He spoke to the Mohawks, and the other Nations seperately from the Oneydoes, because the other Nations were supposed not to have done any Mischief.

"We are come here from Virginia upon occasion of some of your Neighbours doing of Mischief or Harm in our Country, which upon the Interposition and Perswasion of the Governour here, we have wholy passed by and forgiven. And being inform'd, that you are not concern'd therein, but disowning such Actions, we did desire to see you, and to let you know that continuing the like good peaceable Neighbourhood, you shall find us the same, and willing to do you Friendship at all times, but we must acquaint you, that we have a Law, &c." (repeating the same words which he spoke to the Oneydoes on that subject.)

On the Twentyfifth, he thought it necessary to repeat this last Speech to the Mohawks by themselves, who after they had receiv'd some Presents, answered on the Twentysixth before Noon,

"WE are glad to see you here, and to speak with you in this place, where we never saw you before. We understood your

Propositions; We thank you for your Presents and shall give you an Answer Afternoon.

In the Afternoon they said,

"Bretheren;

"You have had no small trouble to come hither from Virginia, for it is a long Journey. We are at your request, and with our Governors Consent, come to meet you in this House, which is appointed for our Treaties, to hear you speak, and to give you an Answer. But before we give an Answer, we make the appointed House clean by giving this (*k*) Fathom of Wampum.

"We just now said, that your long Journey must have not been without much Fatigue, especially to you who are an Old Man. I am old likewise, and therefore I give you this Fathom of Wampum to mitigate your pain.

"In the Beginning of your Speech you tell us of the League or Covenant made with Coll. Coursey. We remember it very well, that it was made in our Governors Presence. We have kept it hitherto, and are resolv'd to keep it Inviolably. We are glad to see you here, to renew this Covenant. You do better than the People of the East, (New-England) who made a Covenant at the same time; for we have seen none of them since, to renew and keep up the Remembrance of it. Then they gave a Fathom of Wampum.

"We have said what we have to say, as to the Covenant made with Coll. Coursey. You desire us likewise to continue our good Neighbourhood. This we not only promise to do, but likewise to keep the (*l*) Chain, which cannot be broken, clean and bright, and therefore we desire you to do the same. Then gave a Belt of Wampum twelve deep.

(*k*) A Fathom of Wampum is a single string of Wampum of that length, it is of less value than the Belts, and therefore given in Matters of smaller Consequence; and by cleaning the House, they mean putting away Hypocresy and Deceit.

(*l*) The Indians always express a League by a Chain by which two or more things are kept fast together.

"We are glad that by the Interposition and Perswasion of our Governor, the Mischeif which our Neighbours did in your Country is passed over, and now wholly forgiven. Let it be buried in Oblivion; for if any mischief should befal them (seeing we make but one body with them,) we must have partaken with them. We approve of your Law, to lay down our Arms as a token of Friendship, and we shall do so for the future. Then gave a Belt fourteen deep.

"We were told before we heard your Propositions, that one of the Agents from Virginia was Dead. We lament and bewail his Death, but admire that nothing was laid down, according to our Custom, when the Death of such a Person was signified to us. We give you this Belt of Black Wampum (thirteen deep) to wipe away your Tears."

The Onnondagas did not come till November, on the 5th of which Month the Virginia Agent spoke to them in the same words he had done to the Oneydoes. None of their Answers appear upon the Registers, except the Mohawks, which we have given. It is certain that the Onnondagas and Oneydoes did not observe the Peace with Virginia, but molested them with the reiterated Incursions of their Parties. It is observable however, that these two Nations and the Cayugas only, had received French Priests among them, and that none of the rest who were not under the Influence of those Priests, ever molested the English; for which reason Coll. Dongan, tho' a Papist, complained of the ill Offices the Priests did to the English Interest, and forbid the Five Nations to entertain any of them, tho' the English and French Crowns, while he was Governor of New-York, in King James's Reign, seem'd to be more than ever in strict Friendship.

The French could have no hopes of perswading the Indians to hurt any of the Inhabitants of New-York, but they were in hopes, that by the Indian Parties doing frequently Mischief in Virginia, the Government of New-York would be forced to joyn in resenting the Injury, and thereby that Union between the Government of New-York and the Five Nations would be broke, which always obstructed and often defeated the Designs of the French, to subject all North-America to the Crown of France. For this reason the Governors of New-York have always, with the greatest Caution, avoided a Breach with these Nations, on account of the little Differences they had with the Neighbouring Colonys.

These new Incursions of these two Nations were so troublesome to the People of Virginia, that their Governor, the Lord Howard of Effingham, thought it necessary for their Security, to undertake a Voyage to New-York.

The Sachems of the Five Nations being call'd to Albany, his Lordship met there eight Mohawk, three Oneydoe, three Onnondaga and three Cayuga Sachems, and on the Thirtieth of July, 1684. being accompanied with two of the Council of Virginia, he spoke to them as follows, in the presence of Col. Thomas Dongan, Governor of New-York, two of the Council of New-York, and the Magistrates of Albany. The Sennekas living far off were not then arriv'd.

Propositions made by the Right Honourable Francis Lord Howard of Effingham, Governor General of His Majesty's Dominion of Virginia,

To the Mohawks, Oneydoes, Onnondagas and Cayugas.

"It is now about seven years ago since you (unprovok'd) came into Virginia, a Country belonging to the Great King of England, and committed several Murders and Robberys, carrying away our Christian Women and Children Prisoners into your Castles. All which Injurys we designed to have Revenged on you; but at the desire of Sir Edmond Andross, then Governor General of this Country, we desisted from destroying you, and sent our Agents Col. William Kendall and Col. Southley Littleton, to Confirm and make sure the Peace that Col. Coursey of Maryland included us in, when first he

Treated with you. We find, that as you quickly forgot what you promised Col. Coursey, so you have willfully broke the Covenant Chain, which you promised our Agent, Col. Kendall, should be most strong and bright, if we of Virginia, would bury in the Pit of Oblivion, the Injurys you had then done us, which upon your Governor Andross's Intercession, and your Submission, we were willing to forget; But you not at all minding the Covenant then made, have every year since, come into our Country, in a War-like manner, under pretence of Fighting with our Indians, our Friends and Neighbours, which you ought not to have done, our Agent having encluded them likewise in the Peace. You not only destroyed and took many of them Prisoners, but you have also kill'd and burnt our Christian People, destroying our Corn and Tobacco, more than you made use of, killing our Horses, Hogs and Cattle, not to eat, but let them ly in the Woods and stink. This you did, when you were not denyed anything you said you wanted.

"I must also tell you that under the pretence of Friendship, you have come to our Houses at the heads of our Rivers (where they have been fortified) with a white Sheet on a Pole, and have laid down your Guns before the Fort, upon which our People taking you to be Friends, have admitted your great Men into their Forts, and have given them Meat and Drink, what they desired. After the great Men had refreshed themselves, and desiring to return, as they were let out of the Fort Gates, the young Men rushed into the Fort and plunder'd the House, taking away and destroying all the Corn, Tobacco, Bedding, and what else was in the House. When they went away, they took several Sheep with them, and kill'd several Cows big with Calf, and left them behind them, cut to pieces and flung about, as if it were in Defiance of the Peace, and destroying of our Friendship.

"These, and many more Injurys that you have done us, have caused me to raise Forces, to send to the heads of our Rivers to defend our People from your Outrages, till I came to

New-York to Col. Thomas Dongan, your Governor General, to desire him, as we are all one Kings Subjects, to assist me in Warring against you, to Revenge the Christian Blood that you have shed, and to make you give full Satisfaction for all the goods that you destroyed. But by the Mediation of your Governor, I am now come to Albany to speak with you, and to know the reason of your breaking the Covenant Chain, not only with us and our neighbour Indians but with Maryland, who are great King Charles's Subjects; for our Indians have giv'n great King Charles their Land. Therefore I, the Governor of Virginia, will protect them, as your Governor under the Great Duke of York and Albany; will henceforth you, when the Chain of Friendship is made between us all.

"Now that I have let you know that I am sensible of all the Injurys that you have done us, by the desire of your noble Governor General, I am willing to make a new Chain with you for Virginia, Maryland, and our Indians, that may be more strong and lasting, even to the World's end, so that we may all be Bretheren and Great King Charles's Children.

"I propose to you, *First,* That you call out of our Countrys of Virginia and Maryland all your young Men or Soldiers that are now there.

"*Secondly,* That you do not hinder or molest our Friend Indians from Hunting at our Mountains, it having been their Country and none of yours. They never go into your Country to disturb any of you.

"*Thirdly,* Tho' the Damages you have done our Country be very great, and would require a great deal of Satisfaction, which you are bound to give, yet we assure you, that only by the Perswasions of your Governor, who is at a vast deal of Trouble and Charge for your Wellfare, which you ever ought to acknowledge, I have passed it by and forgiven you, upon this Condition, that your People, nor any living among you, never commit any Incursions on our Christians or Indians living among us, or in Maryland.

"For the better Confirmation of the same and that the

Peace now concluded, may be lasting, I propose to have two (*m*) Hatchets buried as a final Determination of all Wars and Jarrings between us: One on behalf of us and our Indians, and the other for all your Nations united together, that ever did us any Injury, or pretended to War against our Indian Friends or Maryland.

"And that nothing may be wanting for Confirmation thereof, (if you desire it) we are willing to send some of our Indian Sachems with an Agent next Summer, about this time, that they may Ratifie the Covenant with you here in this prefixed House, where you may see and speak together as Friends.

"That the Covenant now made between us in this prefixed House, in the presence of your Governor, may be firmly kept and perform'd on your parts, as it always has on ours, and that you do not break any one Link of the Covenant Chain for the future, by your Peoples coming near our Plantations; When you march to the Southward, keep to the feet of the Mountains, and not come nigh the heads, of our Rivers, there being no Bever Hunting there; for we shall not for the future (tho' you lay down your Arms as Friends) ever trust you more, you have so often deceiv'd us."

The next Day the Mohawks answered first by their Speaker, saying,

"We must, in the first place, say something to the other three Nations by way of Reproof for their not keeping the former Covenant, as they ought, and therefore we desire you, great Sachem of Virginia, and you Corlaer, and all People here present, to hearken, for we will conceal nothing of the Evil they have done.

(Then turning to the other three Nations) "You have heard Yesterday all that has been said; as for our parts, we are free

(*m*) All Indians make use of the Hatchet or Ax as an emblem to express War.

of the blame laid on us for the Mischief done in Virginia and Maryland. You are Stupid, Brutish, and have no Understanding, thus to break your Covenant. We have always been obedient to Corlaer, and have steadily kept our Covenant with Virginia, Maryland and Boston; we must therefore Stamp Understanding into you. Let the Covenant made Yesterday, be carefully kept for the future. This we earnestly recommend to you; for we are ready to cry, for shame of you. Let us be no more ashamed on your Account, but be obedient, and take this Belt to keep what we say in your Remembrance.

"Hear now, now is the time to hearken. The Covenant Chain had very near slipt. You have not observ'd your Covenant. Observe it now, when all former Evil is buried in the Pit.

"You Oneydoes, I speak to you as (n) Children. Be no longer void of Understanding.

"You Onnondagas, our Bretheren, you are like Deaf People, that cannot hear, your Senses are cover'd with Dirt and Filth.

"You Cayugas, Do not return into your former ways. There are three things we must all observe.

"*First,* The Covenant with Corlaer. *Secondly,* The Covenant with Virginia and Maryland. *Thirdly,* The Covenant with Boston. We must Stamp Understanding into you, that you may be obedient. And Take this Belt for a Remembrancer."

Then Odianne, the same Mohawk Speaker, turning to my Lord, spoke in behalf of all the four Nations.

"We are very thankful to you, great Sachem of Virginia, that you are pleased to be perswaded by Corlaer, our Governor, to forgive all former Faults. We are very glad to hear you and to see your Heart softned. Take these three Bevers as a Token.

"We thank the great Sachem of Virginia for saying, that

(n) The Mohawks always call the Oneydoes Children, and the Oneydoes acknowledge the Mohawks to be their Fathers.

the Ax shall be thrown into the Pit. Take these two Bevers as a Token of our Joy and Thankfulness.

"We are glad that (*o*) Assarigoa, will bury in the Pit what is past, and stamp thereon. Let a strong stream likewise run under the Pit, to wash the evil all away. *Gives 2 Bevers.*

"My Lord, you are a Man of great Knowledge and Understanding, thus to keep the Covenant Chain bright as Silver, and now again to Renew it, and make it stronger.

(Then pointing to the other three Nations said,) "But they are Covenant Breakers. I lay down this as a Token that we Mohawks have kept the Covenant entire on our parts. Giving two Bevers and a Raccoon.

"The Covenant must be kept; for the fire of Love of Virginia and Maryland burns in this place, as well as ours, and this Covenant House must be kept clean. Gives two Bevers.

"We now plant a (*p*) Tree, who's tops will reach the Sun, and its Branches spread far abroad, so that it shall be seen afar off; & we shall shelter ourselves under it, and live in Peace, without molestation. Gives two Bevers.

"You proposed yesterday, that if we were desirous to see the Indians of Virginia, you are willing to send some of their Sachems next Summer about this time to this Place. This Proposal pleases us very much. The sooner they come, it will be the better, that we may speak with them in this House, which is apointed for our speaking with our Friends. And gave two Belts to confirm it.

"You have now heard what Exhortation we have made to the other three Nations. We have taken the Hatchet out of their hands. We now therefore pray, that your Hatchet may likewise be buried in the Pit. Giving two Bevers,

"Let the River be secure, for we sometimes make Propositions to the Raritan and Nevessink Indians; but above all, let

(*o*) The Name, which the Five Nations always give the Governors of Virginia.

(*p*) The Five Nations always express Peace under the Metapher of a Tree, in this manner.

your Virginia Indians come securely hither, that we may keep a good Correspondence with them.

"My Lord, Some of us Mohawks are out against Our Enemies that live a far off. When they come near your Plantations, they will do you no harm, nor Plunder as the others do. Be kind to them, if they shall happen to come to any of your Plantations. Give them some Tobacco and some Victuals; for they will neither Rob nor Steal, as the Oneydoes, Onnondagas and Cayugas have done.

"The Oneydoes particularly Thank your Lordship for hearkening to lay down the Ax. The Hatchet is taken out of all their hands. And gives a Belt.

"We again thank your Lordship, that the Covenant Chain is Renewed. Let it be kept clean and bright, and held fast, Let not any one pull his Arm from it. We enclude all the Four Nations in giving this Belt.

"We again pray your Lordship, to take the Oneydoes into your Friendship, and that you keep the Covenant Chain strong with them; for they are in our Covenant." Gives a Belt.

The Oneydoes give twenty Bevers, as satisfaction for what they promised my Lord Baltimore, and desire that they may be Discharged.

My Lord and the Governor told them, That they would use their Endeavours with the Lord Baltimore, to perswade him to forgive what remained.

Then the Indians desired that the Hole might be digged, to bury the Axes, *viz.* One in behalf of Virginia and their Indians, another in behalf of Maryland and their Indians, and three for the Oneydoes, Onnondagas and Cayugas. The Mohawks said, there was no need of burying any on their Account; for the first Chain had never been broke by them.

Then the three Nations spoke by an Onnondaga, call'd Thanohjanihta, who said,

"We Thank the great Sachem of Virginia, that he has so readily forgiven and forgot the Evil that has been done; And We, on our parts, gladly catch at, and lay hold of the Chain."

Then each of them deliver an Ax to be buried, and gave a Belt.

The Speaker added, "I speak in the Name of all three Nations, and include them in this Chain, which we desire may be kept clean and bright like Silver. Gives a Belt.

"We desire that the Path may be open for the Indians, under your Lordships Protection to come safely and freely to this place, in order to confirm this Peace." Gives six Fathom of Wampum.

Then the Axes were buried in the Southeast end of the Court-yard, and the Indians threw the Earth upon them. After which my Lord told them, *That since now a firm Peace was concluded, We shall hereafter remain Friends, and Virginia and Maryland will send once in two or three years to Renew it, and some of Our Indian Sachems shall come, according to your desire, to Confirm it.*

Last of all, the Oneydoes, Onnondagas and Cayugas, joyntly, sang the Peace Song, with Demonstrations of much Joy; and Thank'd the Governor of New-York for his effectual Mediation with the Governor of Virginia, in their favour.

The Mohawks by themselves, and the other three Nations by themselves, spoke to the Governor of New-York, much to the same purpose that they did to the Governor of Virginia, so far as it related to the Affair of Virginia, but with some particular Marks of Personal Esteem; for he had won their Affections by his former carriage towards them. And they desired the Duke of York's Arms to put upon their Castles. Which, we may suppose, they were told, would save them from the French.

Coll. Dongan desired them to call home those of their Nations that had settled in Canada. (*q*) To which they answered,

(*q*) The French Priests had (from time to time) perswaded several of the Five Nations to leave their own Country, and to settle near Montreal,

"Corlaer keeps a Correspondence with Canada, and therefore he can prevail more than we can. Let Corlaer use his endeavours to draw our Indians home to their own Country." And gave a Bever.

At the same Time, the Government of the Massachusets-Bay had appointed Coll. Stephanus Cortlandt, one of the Council of New-York, their Agent, to Renew their Covenant with the Five Nations, and to give them some small Presents: Which was accordingly done.

The Governor of New-York, Coll. Dongan, concluded all, with this Advice to them, *Keep a good Understanding among your Selves: If any Difference should happen, acquaint me with it, and I will compose it. Make no Covenant or Agreement with the French, or any other Nation, without my Knowledge or Approbation.* Then he gave the Dukes Arms, to be put upon each of their Castles, in hopes it might deter the French from attacking them (as they were threaten'd from Canada) after they had so manifestly declared themselves to be under the Protection of the Crown of England.

Before I proceed further it will be necessary to incert a Remarkable Speech made by the Onnondagas and Cayugas, to the two Governors, on the 2d day of August, *viz.*

"Brother Corlaer;

"Your Sachem is a great Sachem, and We are but a small People. But when the English came first to Manhatan, (*r*) Aragiske, (*s*) and to Yakokranagary, (*t*) they were then but a Small People, and we Great. Then, because we found you a

---

where the French are very industrious in encouraging them. Their Numbers have been likewise encreased by the Prisoners the French have taken in War, and by others who have run from their own Country, because of some Mischief that they had done, or Debts which they ow'd to the Christians. These Indians all profess Christianity, and therefore are commonly call'd The Praying Indians by their Country-men, and they are called Cahnuagas by the People of Albany.

(*r*) New-York.   (*s*) Virginia.   (*t*) Maryland.

good People, we treated you civilly, and gave you Land. We hope therefore, now that you are Great and we Small, you will protect us from the French. If you do not, we shall loose all our Hunting, and our Bevers. The French will get all the Bever. They are now angry with us, because we carry our Bever to our Brethren.

"We have put our Lands and our Selves under the Protection of the great Duke of York, the Brother of your great Sachem, who is likewise a great Sachem.

"We have given the Susquehana River, which We won with the Sword, to this Government, and we desire that it may be a Branch of the great Tree that grows in this Place, the top of which reaches the Sun, and its Branches shelter us from the French, and all other Nations. Our Fire burns in your Houses, and your Fire burns with us. We desire that it may always be so.

"We will not that any of the great Penn's People settle upon the Susquehana River; for we have no other Land to leave to our Children.

"Our young People are Soldiers, and when they are disobliged they are like Wolves in the Woods, as you Sachem of Virginia very well know.

"We have put our Selves under the great Sachem Charles, that lives on the other side of the great Lake. We give you these two White drest Deer-Skins to be sent to the great Sachem, that he may write on them, and put a great Red Seal to them, to Confirm what We now do, and put the Susquehana River above the Wasuhta (*u*) and all the rest of our Land under the great Duke of York, and give that Land to no body else. Our Brethren, his People, have been like Fathers to our Wives and Children, and have given us Bread, when we were in need of it: We will not therefore joyn our selves or our Lands to any other Government but this. We desire Corlaer, our Governor, may send over this Proposition to the great Sachem, Charles, who dwells on the other side

(*u*) The Falls.

the great Lake, with this Belt of Wampum, and this other smaller Belt to the Duke of York, his Brother; And we give you, Corlaer, this Beaver, to send over this Proposition.

"You great Man of Virginia, We let you know, that great Penn did speak to us here in Corlaers House, by his Agents, and desired to buy the Susquehana River of us, but we would not hearken to him; for we had fasten'd it to this Government. We desire of you therefore, that you would bear Witness of what we now do, and that we now Confirm what we have done before. Let your Friend, the great Sachem that lives on the other side the great Lake, know this, that We being a Free People, tho' united to the English, may give our Lands, and be joyn'd to the Sachem we like best. We give this Bever to Remember what we say."

The Senekas arrived soon after, and on the 5th of August spoke to my Lord Howard in the following manner.

"WE have heard and understood what Mischief hath been done in Virginia. We have it as perfect as if it were upon our Fingers ends. O Corlaer! We Thank you for having been our Intercessor, so that the Ax hath not fallen upon Us.

"And you, Assarigoa, great Sachem of Virginia, We Thank you for burying all Evil in the Pit. We are inform'd, that the Mohawks, Oneydoes, Onnondagas and Cayugaes have buried the Ax already; Now we that live the remotest off, are come to do the same, and to include in this Chain the Cahnawaas, your Friends, who live amongst you. We desire therefore, that an Ax, on our part, may be buried with one of my Lords. O Corlaer! Corlaer! We Thank you for holding one end of the Ax: And We thank you, great Governor of Virginia, not only for throwing aside the Ax, but more especially for your putting all Evil from your Heart. Now we have a New Chain, a strong and a streight Chain that cannot be broken. The Tree of Peace is planted so firmly that it cannot be moved. Let us on both sides hold the Chain fast.

"We understand what you said of the great Sachem that lives on the other side the great Water.

"You tell us, that the Cahnawaas will come hither to strengthen the Chain. Let them not make any Excuse, that they are Old and Feeble, or that their Feet are Sore. If the Old Sachems cannot, let the Young Men come. We shall not fail to come hither, tho' we live the farthest off, and then the New Chain will be stronger and brighter.

"We understand, that because of the Mischief which has been done to the People and Cattle of Virginia and Maryland, we must not come near the Heads of your Rivers, nor near your Plantations, but keep at the foot of the Mountains; for tho' we lay down our Arms, as Friends, we shall not be trusted for the future, but look'd on as Robbers. We agree, however, to this Proposition, and shall wholly stay away from Virginia: And this we do in gratitude to Corlaer, who has been at so great Pains to perswade you, Great Governor of Virginia, to forget what is past. We commend your Understanding, in giving ear to Corlaer's good Advice; and we shall go a path which was never trod before.

"We have now done speaking to Corlaer, and the Governor of Virginia. Let the Chain be forever kept clean and bright, and we shall do the same.

"The other Nations, from the Mohawks Country to the Cayugas, have deliver'd up the Susquehana River, and all that Country, to Corlaer's Government. We Confirm what they have done, by giving this Belt. Ten Bevers are at the Onnondagas Castle in their way hither; We design five of them for Corlaer, and the other five for the Sachem of Virginia."

Coll. Bird, one of the Council of Virginia, and Edmond Jennings, Esq; Attorney General of that Province, came with four Indian Sachems, (according to my Lord Howard's Promise) to Renew and Confirm the Peace, and met the Five Nations at Albany in September, 1685.

Coll. Bird accus'd them of having again broke their Covenant, by taking an Indian Girl from an English Mans House, and four Indian Boys Prisoners.

They excused this, by its being done by the Parties that were out when the Peace was concluded, who knew nothing of it; Which Accidents they had provided against in their Articles. They said, The four Boys were given to the Relations of those Men that were lost, and it would be very difficult to obtain their Restoration. But they promised to deliver them up.

The Senekas and Mohawks declared themselves free of any blame, and chid the other Nations.

So that we may still observe the Influence which the French Priests had obtain'd over those other Nations, and to what Christian-like Purposes they us'd it.

The Mohawks Speaker said, *Where shall I seek the Chain of Peace? Where shall I find it, but upon Our Path? And whither doth Our Path lead us, but unto this House? This is a House of Peace.* And sang all the Covenant Chain over. He afterwards sang by way of Admonition to the Onnondagas, Cayugas and Oneydoes, and concluded all with a Song to the Virginia Indians. But I suppose our Interpreters were not Poets enough to Translate the Songs, otherwise I might have gratified the Reader with a taste of Indian Poetry.

The French Priests still had an Influence over the Onnondagas, Cayugas and Oneydoes, and it was easie for them to spirit up the Indians (naturally Revengeful) against their old Enemies. This occasion'd a Party of the Oneydoes going out two years afterwards against the Wayanoak Indians, Friends of Virginia, and killing some of the People of Virginia, who assisted those Indians. They took six Prisoners, which they restored at Albany, with an Excuse, That they did not know that they were Friends of Virginia, and included in the Chain with Virginia. Coll. Dongan, on this Occasion, told them, That he only had kept all the English in North-America from joyning together to Destroy them; And at the same time threatned them, That if ever he should hear of the like Complaint, he would dig up the Hatchet, and joyn with the rest of the English to cut them off, Root and Branch; for there were many Complaints made of him to the King by the English, as well as the Governor of Canada, for his favouring of them.

Now we have gone through the Material Transactions which the Five Nations had with the English, in which we find the English pursuing nothing but Peaceable and Christian Measures, and the Five Nations (tho' Barbarians) living like good Neighbours and faithful Friends, except when they were influenced by the Arts of the Jesuits; Tho' at the same time one cannot but admire the Zeal, Courage and Resolution of these Jesuits, that would adventure to live among Indians at War with their Nation; and the better to carry their Purposes, to comply with all the Humors and Manners of such a Wild People, so as not to be distinguished by strangers from meer Indians. One of them, nam'd Milet, remain'd with the Oneydoes till after the year 1694. he was advanced to the degree of a Sachem, and had so great an Influence over them, that the other Nations could not prevail with them to part with him. While he remain'd with them, the Oneydoes were frequently turn'd against the Southern Indians (Friends of the English Southern Colonies) and were always wavering in their Resolutions against Canada.

We shall now Return to see what effect the French Policy had, who pursued very different Measures from the English.

CHAP. IV.

Mr. De la Barre's Expedition, and some Remarkable Transactions in 1684.

THE French in the Time they were at Peace with the Five
Nations, built their Fort at Teiodondoraghi or Missilimakinak, and made a Settlement there. They carried their Commerce among the Numerous Nations that live on the Banks of
the great Lakes, and the Banks of the Misissipi. They not only
prosecuted their Trade among these Nations, but did all they
could to secure their Obedience, and to make them absolutely subject to the Crown of France, by building Forts at
the considerable Passes, and placing small Garrisons in them.
They took all the Precautions in their Power, not only to
restrain the Indians by Force, but likewise to gain their Affections, by sending Missionaries among them. The only Obstruction they met with, was from the Five Nations, who introduced the English of New-York into the Lakes, to Trade with
the Indians that liv'd round them. This gave the French much
uneasiness, because they fore-saw, that the English would not
only prove dangerous Rivals, but that the Advantages which
they enjoy'd in Trade, beyond what it was possible for the
Inhabitants of Canada to have, would enable the People of
New-York so far to under-sell them, that their Trade would
soon be Ruin'd, and all the Interest lost which they had gain'd
with so much Labour and Expence. The Five Nations likewise continued in War with many of the Nations, the Chictaghiks particularly, who yielded the most Profitable Trade to the
French; and as often as they discover'd any of the French
carrying Ammunition towards these Nations, they fell upon
them, and took all their Powder, Lead and Arms from them.
This made the French Traders afraid of traveling, and pre-

vented their Indians from hunting, and lessen'd the Opinion they had of the French Power, when they found that the French were not able to protect them against the Insults of the Five Nations.

The Sennekas lie next to the Lakes, and nearest to the Nations with whom the French Traded, and were so averse to the French Nation, that they never would receive any Priest among them, and of consequence were most firmly attached to the English Interest, who supplyed them with Arms and Powder, (the means to be Revenged of their Enemies.) For these reasons Mr. De la Barre (the Governor of Canada) sent a Messenger to Coll. Dongan, to complain of the Injuries the Sennekas had done to the French, and to show the necessity he was under to bring the Five Nations to Reason by Force of Arms; which Messenger happening to arrive at the time the Indians met my Lord Howard at Albany, Coll. Dongan told the Sennekas of the Complaints that the French Governor made of them. They gave him the following Answer, in Presence of Mr. De la Barre's Messenger, on the 5th of August, 1684.

"WE were sent for, and are come, and have heard what you have said to us, That Corlaer hath great Complaints of us, both from Virginia and Canada. What they complain of from Canada, may possibly be true, that our Young People have taken some of their Goods; but Yonnondio is the cause of it. He not only permits his People to carry Ammunition, Guns, Powder, Lead & Axes to the Tuihtuihronoon (x) our Enemys, but sends them thither on purpose. These Guns which he sends knock our Bever-hunters on the head, and our Enemies carry the Bevers to Canada, that we would have brought to our Brethren. Our Bever-hunters are Soldiers, and could bear this no longer. They met with some French in their way to

(x) Ronoon signifies Nation or People, in the Language of the Five Nations, they say Twihtwih-ronoon, Chictaghik-ronoon, Deonondadik-ronoon, &c.

our enemies, and very near them, carrying Ammunition, which our Men took from them. This is agreeable to our Customs of War, and we may therefore openly own it; tho' we know not whether it be practised by the Christians in such like cases.

"When the Governor of Canada speaks to us of the Chain, he calls us Children, and saith, *I am your Father, you must hold fast the Chain, and I will do the same. I will Protect you as a Father doth his Children.* Is this Protection, to speak thus with his Lips, and at the same time to knock us on the head, by assisting our Enemies with Ammunition?

"He always says, *I am your Father, and you are my Children,* and yet he is angry with his Children for taking these goods. But, O Corlaer! O Assarigoa! We must complain to you. You, Corlaer, are a Lord, and Govern this Country; Is it just that our Father is going to fight with us for these things, or is it well done? We rejoyced when La Sal was sent over the great Water, and when Perot was removed, because they had furnished our Enemies with Ammunition; but we are disapointed in our hopes; for we find that our Enemies are still supplied. Is this well done? Yea, he often forbids us to make War on any of the Nations with whom he Trades, and at the same time furnishes them with all sorts of Ammunition, to enable them to destroy us.

"Thus far in Answer to the Complaints which the Governor of Canada hath made of Us to Corlaer. Corlaer said to us, that Satisfaction must be made to the French for the Mischief we have done them. This he said before he heard our Answer. Now let him that hath Inspection over all our Countries, on whom our Eyes are fix'd, let him, ev'n Corlaer judge and determine. If you say it must be paid, we shall pay it, but we cannot live without free Bever-hunting.

"Corlaer, Hear what we say, We Thank you for the Dukes Arms which you have given us to be put on our Castles, as a Defence to them. You command them. Have we wander'd out of the way, as the Governor of Canada says. We do not threaten him with War, as he threatens us. What shall we do? Shall we run away, or shall we sit still in our Houses? What shall we do? We speak to him that Governs and Commands us.

"Now Corlaer and Assarigoa, and all People here present, Remember what we have answered to the Complaints of the Governor of Canada; Yea, let what we say come to his Ears." Then they gave a Belt, and said, there was five Bevers at Onondaga for the Governor.

Mons. De la Barre at this time was gone with all the Force of Canada to Cadarackui Fort, and order'd the three Vessels to be repaired, which the French had built on that Lake. His design was to frighten the Five Nations into his own Terms by the Appearance of so great an Army, which consisted of 600 Soldiers, 400 Indians, and 400 Men that carried Provisions, besides 300 Men that he left to secure Cadarackui Fort. But while he was at this Fort, the Fatigue of Traveling in the Month of August together with the Unhealthiness of that place (the Country thereabout being very Marshy) where he tarryed six weeks, occasioned so great a Sikness in his Army, that he found himself unable to Perform any thing, but by Treaty, and therefore sent Orders to Mons. Dulhut, who was come from Missilimakinak with 600 men French and Indians, to stop. He passed a Cross the Lake with as many men as were able to Travel, and arrived at the River which the French call La Famine, and by the Indians call'd Kaihohage, which runs from the Onnondaga and Oneydo Countrys, and falls into Cadarackui Lakes. There were two Villages of the Five Nations on the North side of the Lake, about five or six Leagues from the French Fort, consisting of those Indians that had the most Inclination to the French: They provided the French Army with Provisions, while they remain'd at the Fort; but it is probable, sent an account to their own Nations of every thing that happen'd, which was the Reason of the Usage they afterwards met with from the French.

When Mr. De la Barre sent to Coll. Dongan, he was in

hopes, from the strict Alliance that was then between the
Crowns of England and France, and from Coll. Dongan's
being a Papist, that he would sit still till he had reduced the
Five Nations. But none of these Reasons permitted that Gentleman to be easie while the French attempted such things, as
in their consequence would be to the highest degree Prejudicial to the English Interest, & put all the English Colonies in
America in danger. Wherefore he dispatch'd the Publick
Interpreter, with Orders to do every thing in his Power to
prevent the Five Nations going to Treat with Mr. De la Barre.

The Interpreter succeeded in his Design with the Mohawks,
and with the Sennekas, who promis'd that they would not go
near the French Governor. But he had not the like Success
with the Onnondagas, Oneydoes and Cayugas, who had receiv'd the French Priests. For they would not hear the Interpreter, but in Presence of the French Priest, and of Mr. Le
Maine, whom the Indians call Ohquesse (*y*) and three other
French Men, that Mr. De la Barre had sent to perswade them
to meet him at Kaihohage, ten Leagues from the Onnondaga
Castle. They gave the following Answer to the Interpreter.

"Arie, You are Corlaer's Messenger? Ohquesse is the Governor of Canada's; and there sits our Father (*z*). Yonnondio
acquainted us some time ago, that he would speak with us
before he would undertake any thing against the Sennakas.
Now he hath sent for all the Nations to speak with him in
Friendship, and that at a Place not far from Onnondaga, ev'n
at Kaihohage. But our Brother Corlaer tells us, That we must
not meet the Governor of Canada without his Permission; and
that if Yonnondio have any thing to say to us, he must first
send to Corlaer for leave to speak with us. Yonnondio has sent
long ago to us to speak with him, and he has lately repeated
that Desire, by Onnissantie, the Brother of our Father Twir-
haersira, that sits there. He has not only intreated us by our
Father, but by two Praying Indians, one an Onnondaga, the

(*y*) That is, the Partridge.   (*z*) Pointing to the Jesuit.

other the Son of an Old Mohawk Sachem, Connondowe. They brought five great Belts of Wampum, not a Fathom or two only, as you bring. Now Ohquesse has been sent with three French-men: Yonnondio not content with all this, has likewise sent Dennehoot, and two other Mohawks to perswade us to meet him, and to speak with him of good Things. Should we not go to him, after all this Entreaty, when he is come so far, and so near to us, certainly if we do not, we shall provoke his Wrath, and not deserve this Goodness. You say we are Subjects to the King of England and Duke of York, but we say, we are Brethren. We must take care of our selves. Those Arms fixed upon the Post without the Gate, cannot defend us against the Arms of La Barre.

"Brother Corlaer, We tell you, That we shall bind a Covenant Chain to our Arm, and to his, as thick as that Post (*Pointing to a Post of the House*) "Be not dissatisfi'd; should we not imbrace this Happiness offer'd to us, *viz.* Peace, in the place of War; yea, we shall take the Evil doers, the Sennekas by the hand, and La Barre likewise, and their ax and his Sword shall be thrown into a deep Water. We wish our Brother Corlaer were present, but it seems the time will not permit of it."

Accordingly Garangula, one of the chief Sachems of the Onnondagas, with thirty Warriors, went with Mr. Le Maine to meet the Governor of Canada at Kaihohage. After he had remain'd two Days in the French Camp Mr. La Barre spoke to him, as follows, (the French Officers making a Semi-circle on one side while Garangula, with his Warriors, compleated the Circle on the other.)

(*b*) *Mons. De La Barre's Speech to Garangula.*

"The King, my Master, being inform'd that the Five Nations have often infring'd the Peace, has order'd me to come hither

(*b*) Voyages du Baron de la Hontan, Tome 1. Lettre 7.

with a Guard, and to send Ohquesse to the Onnondagas to bring the chief Sachems to my Camp. The Intention of the great King is, that you and I may smoke the Calumet (*c*) of Peace together, but on this Condition, that you Promise me, in the Name of the Sennekas, Cayugas, Onnondagas, Oneydoes and Mohawks, to give entire Satisfaction and Reparation to his Subjects, and for the future never to molest them.

"The Sennekas, Cayugas, Onnondagas, Oneydoes and Mohawks have Rob'd and Abus'd all the Traders that were passing towards the Illinois and Umamies, and other Indian Nations, the Children of my King. They have acted, on these occasions, contrary to the Treaty of Peace with my Predecessor. I am order'd therefore to demand Satisfaction, and to tell them, That in case of Refusal, or their Plundering us any more, that I have express Orders to declare War. *This Belt Confirms my Words.*

"The Warriors of the Five Nations have conducted the English into the Lakes, which belong to the King, my Master, and brought the English among the Nations that are his Children, to destroy the Trade of his Subjects, and to withdraw those Nations from him. They have carried the English thither notwithstanding the Prohibition of the late Governor of New-York, who fore-saw the Risque that both they and you would run. I am willing to forget these things, but if ever the like shall happen for the future, I have express Orders to declare War against you. *This Belt Confirms my Words.*

"Your Warriors have made several Barbarous Incursions on the Ilinois and Umamies. They have Massacreed Men,

(*c*) The Calumet is a large Smoking Pipe, made of Marble, most commonly of a dark Red, well polished, shaped some-what in the form of a Hatchet, and adorned with large Feathers of several Colours. It is used in all the Indian Treatyes with Strangers, as a Flag of Truce between contending Partys, which all the Indians think a very high Crime to violate. These Calumets are generally of nice Workmanship, and were in use before the Indians knew any thing of the Christians; for which Reason we are at a loss to conceive by what means they pierced these Pipes and shaped them so finely, before they had the use of Iron.

Women and Children, and have made many of these two Nations Prisoners, who thought themselves safe in their Villages, in time of Peace. These People, who are my Kings Children, must not be your Slaves, you must give them their Liberty, and send them back into their own Country. If the Five Nations shall refuse to do this, I have express Orders to declare War against them. *This Belt Confirms my Words.*

"This is what I had to say to Garangula, that he may carry to the Sennekas, Cayugas, Onnondagas, Oneydoes and Mohawks the Declaration which the King, my Master, has commanded me to make. He doth not wish them to force him to send a great Army to Cadarackui Fort, to begin a War, which must be fatal to them. He would be sorry that this Fort, which was the Work of Peace, should become the Prison of your Warriors. We must endeavour, on both sides, to prevent such Misfortunes. The French, who are the Brethren and Friends of the Five Nations, will never trouble their repose, Provided that the Satisfaction which I demand, be given, and that the Treatyes of Peace be hereafter observed. I shall be extreamly grieved if my words do not produce the Effect which I expect from them; for then I shall be obliged to joyn with the Governor of New-York, who is Commanded by his Master to assist me, and burn the Castles of the Five Nations, and destroy you. *This Belt Confirms my Words.*"

Garangula was very much surprized to find the soft words of the Jesuit, and of the Governors Messengers, turn'd to such threatning Language. They were designed to strike Terror into the Indians. But Garangula having had good information, from those of the Five Nations living near Cadarackui Fort, of all the Sickness and other Misfortunes which attended the French Army, they were far from producing the designed Effect. All the time that Mons. De la Barre spoke, Garangula kept his Eyes fixed upon the end of his Pipe. And as soon as the Governor had done speaking, he rose up, and having walked five or six times round the Circle, he returned to his place, where he spoke standing, while Mons. De la Barre kept his Elbow Chair, and said,

Garangula's Answer.

"Yonnondio, I Honour you, and the Warriors that are with me all likewise honour you. Your Interpreter has finished your Speech; I now begin mine. My words make haste to reach your Ears, hearken to them.

"Yonnondio, You must have believed when you left Quebeck, that the Sun had burnt up all the Forests which render our Country Unaccessible to the French, Or that the Lakes had so far overflown their Banks, that they had surrounded our Castles, and that it was impossible for us to get out of them. Yes, Yonnondio, surely you must have thought so, and the Curiosity of seeing so great a Country burnt up, or under Water, has brought you so far. Now you are undeceived, since that I and my Warriors are come to assure you that the Sennekas, Cayugas, Onnondagas, Oneydoes and Mohawks are all alive. I thank you, in their Name, for bringing back into their Country the Calumet which your Predecessor received from their hands. It was happy for you that you left under ground that Murdering Hatchet which has been so often dyed in the Blood of the French. Hear Yonnondio, I do not Sleep, I have my eyes Open, and the Sun which enlightens me discovers to me a great Captain at the head of a Company of Soldiers, who speaks as if he were Dreaming. He says that he only came to the Lake to smoke on the great Calumet with the Onnondagas. But Garangula says, that he sees the Contrary, that it was to knock them on the head, if Sickness had not weakned the Arms of the French.

"I see Yonnondio Raving in a Camp of sick men, who's Lives the great Spirit has saved, by Inflicting this Sickness on them. Hear Yonnondio, Our Women had taken their Clubs, our Children and Old Men had carried their Bows and Arrows into the heart of your Camp, if our Warriors had not disarmed them, and retained them when your Messenger, Ohquesse appeared in our Castle. It is done, and I have said it.

"Hear Yonnondio, we plundered none of the French, but those that carried Guns, Powder and Ball to the Twihtwies and Chictaghicks, because those Arms might have cost us our Lives. Herein we follow the example of the Jesuits, who stave all the Barrels of Rum brought to our Castle, lest the Drunken Indians should knock them on the Head. Our Warriors have not Bevers enough to pay for all these Arms that they have taken, and our Old Men are not afraid of the War. *This Belt preserves my Words.*

"We carried the English into our Lakes, to traffick there with the Utawawas and Quatoghies, as the Adirondacks brought the French to our Castles, to carry on a Trade which the English say is theirs. We are born free, We neither depend upon Yonnondio nor Corlaer.

"We may go where we please, and carry with us whom we please, and buy and sell what we please. If your Allies be your Slaves, use them as such, Command them to receive no other but your People. *This Belt Preserves my Words.*

"We knockt the Twihtwies and Chictaghiks on the head, because they had cut down the Trees of Peace, which were the Limits of our Country. They have hunted Bevers on our Lands: They have acted contrary to the Custom of all Indians; for they left none of the Bevers alive, they kill'd both Male and Female. They brought the Satanas (*d*) into their Country, to take part with them, and Arm'd them, after they had concerted ill Designs against us. We have done less than either the English or French, that have usurp'd the Lands of so many Indian Nations, and chased them from their own Country. *This Belt Preserves my Words.*

"Hear Yonondio, What I say is the Voice of all the Five Nations. Hear what they Answer, Open your Ears to what they Speak. The Sennekas, Cayugas, Onnondagas, Oneydoes and Mohawks say, That when they buried the Hatchet at

(*d*) Called Sawonons by the French.

Cadarackui (in the presence of your Predecessor) in the middle
of the Fort, they planted the Tree of Peace, in the same place,
to be there carefully preserved, that, in place of a Retreat
for Soldiers, that Fort might be a Rendevouze of Merchants;
that in place of Arms and Munitions of War, Bevers and Merchandize should only enter there.

"Hear, Yonondio, Take care for the future, that so great a
Number of Soldiers as appear here do not choak the Tree of
Peace planted in so small a Fort. It will be a great Loss, if after
it had so easily taken root, you should stop its growth, and
prevent its covering your Country and ours with its Branches.
I assure you, in the Name of the Five Nations, That our Warriors shall dance to the Calumet of Peace under its leaves,
and shall remain quiet on their Mats, and shall never dig up
the Hatchet till their Brethren, Yonnondio or Corlaer shall
either joyntly or seperately endeavour to attack the Country
which the great Spirit has given to our Ancestors. *This Belt
preserves my Words, and this other, the Authority which the
Five Nations have given me.*"

Then Garangula addressing himself to Mr. Le Main, said,
"Take Courage, Ohquesse, you have Spirit, Speak, Explain
my Words, Forget nothing, Tell all that your Brethren and
Friends say to Yonnondio, your Governor, by the Mouth of
Garangula, who honours you, and desires you to accept of this
Present of Bever, and take part with me in my Feast, to which
I invite you. This Present of Bevers is sent to Yonnondio on
the part of the Five Nations."

When Garangula's Harrangue was explain'd to Mr. De la
Barre, he return'd to his Tent, enraged at what he had heard.

Garangula feasted the French Officers, and then Return'd.
And Mons. De la Barre set out in in his way towards Montreal.
As soon as the General was embarqued with the few Soldiers
that remain'd in Health, the Militia made the best of their
way to their own Habitations, without any Order or Discipline.

Thus a very Chargeable and Fatiguing Expedition (which was to strike the Terror of the French Name into the Stubborn Hearts of the Five Nations) ended by a Dispute between the French General and an Old Indian.

When the Indians came to Albany, after they had met with Mr. De la Barre, (and were upbraided for it by Coll. Dongan) Carachkondie, and Onnondaga, slyly answer'd, *We are sorry, and ashamed; for now we understand that the Governor of Canada is not so great a Man as the English King that lives on the other side the great Water; and we are vexed for having given the Governor of Canada so many fine Wampum Belts.*

CHAP. V.

The English Attempt to Trade in the Lakes, and Mr. De Nonville Attacks the Sennekas.

MONSIEUR Le Marquis de Nonville having succeeded Mr. De la Barre, in 1685. and having brought a considerable Reinforcement of Soldiers with him, he resolv'd to Recover the Honour the French had lost in the last Expedition, and to Revenge the Slaughter that the Five Nations continued to make of the Twihtwiks and Chictaghiks, who had put themselves under the Protection of the French; for the Five Nations having entirely subdued the Chicktaghiks, (*e*) after a six years War, they resolv'd next to fall upon the Twihtwies, and to call them to an account for the Disturbance they had given some of the Five Nations in their Bever-hunting. The Five Nations have few or no Bevers in their own Country, and are for that reason obliged to hunt at a great distance, which often occasion'd Disputes with their Neighbours about the Property of the Bever, in some parts of the Country. The Bevers are the

(*e*) Called Ilinois by the French.

most valuable part of the Indian Trade. And as the Twihtwies carried their Bever to the French, the English favour'd the Five Nations in these Expeditions, and particularly in the beginning of the year 1687, made the Five Nations a Present of a Barrel of Powder, when their whole Force was preparing to go against the Twihtwies. The English were the better pleas'd with this War, because they thought it would divert their Thoughts from the Indians that were friends to Virginia: But the French were resolv'd to Support their Friends more effectually by a powerful Diversion, and to change the Seat of the War.

For this purpose Mr. De Nonville sent, in May, 1687, great Quantities of Provisions to Cadarackui Fort, and gather'd the whole Force of Canada to Montreal. His Army consisted of 1500 French of the Regular Troops & Militia, and 500 Indians that lived near Montreal and Quebeck.

He sent likewise Orders to the Commandant at Missilimaki-nak to assemble all the Nations round him, and to March them to Oniagara, in order to joyn the Forces of Canada design'd against the Sennekas. And the other Officers posted among the Indians Westward, had the like Orders.

The Twihtwies receiv'd the Hatchet with joy, from the hands of the French Officer, against the Five Nations. The Outagamies (f) Kikabous, and Maskoutuhs, who were not us'd to Cannoes, were at first perswaded to joyn the Twihtwies, who were to march by Land to Teuchsagrondie, where there was a French Fort, at which they were to be supply'd with Ammunition: But after the French Officer left them, the Utagamies and Maskuticks were disswaded by some of the Mahikander Indians, who happen'd to be with a neighbouring Nation at that time.

The Putewatemies, Malhominies and Puans offer'd them-selves willingly, and went to the Rendevouze at Missilimaki-nak, where they were receiv'd by the Utawawas with all the

(f) The Outagamies, Kikabons, Malhominies and Puans live on the West side of Lake Michigan.

Marks of Honour usually paid to Soldiers, tho' the Utawawas had no inclination to the present Enterprize; they could not tell, however, how to appear against it, otherwise than by inventing what Delays they could to prevent their Marching.

In the mean while, a Cannoe arriv'd, which was sent by Mr. De Nonville with his Orders to the Officers. This Cannoe in her Passage discover'd some English commanded by Major McGregory, in their way to Teiodondaraghie. The English thought (after they had an account of the new Alliance their King had enter'd into with the French) that the French would not disturb them in prosecuting a Trade with the Indians every where, and that the Trade would be equally free and open to both Nations. With these hopes a considerable Number of Adventurers, went out under the Conduct of Major M'Gregory to Trade with the Indians living on the Banks of the Lakes; and that they might be the more wellcome, perswaded the Five Nations to set all the Dionondadie Prisoners at Liberty, who went along with the English and conducted them towards Missilimakinak or Teiodondoraghie. But the English found themselves mistaken, for the French Commandant at Teiodondoraghie, as soon as he had Notice of this, sent 300 French to intercept the English.

(g) The Utawawas and Dionondadies having likewise an account of the English, designed to support their own Independency, and to encourage the English Trade. The Return of the Dionondadie Prisoners made that Nation very hearty in favouring the English, they therefore marched immediately off, with design to joyn Major M'Gregory, but the Utawawas were divided in their Inclinations, their Chief, with about thirty more joyn'd the French, the rest remain'd in suspence and stood Neuter.

The Utawawas thus wavering, disconcerted the Measures of the Deionondadies, for they began to suspect the Utawawas, and therefore immediately return'd to secure their Wives and

(g) Histoire de Le Amerique Septentrionale par Mr. De la Poterie, Tome 2. Chap. 16.

Children they had left near the French Fort with the Utawa-was. The English and their Effects were seized without any Opposition, and were carried to the French fort at Teio-dondoraghie.

The English brought great Quantities of Rum with them, (which the Indians love more than their Life) and the French being afraid that if the Indians took to drinking, they would grow ungovernable, did what they could to keep them from it. They were most concerned that the Putewatemies, (who had no knowledge of the English, or of that bewitching Liquor, and were firmly attached to the French) should not taste it.

The Utawawas still contrived delays to the March, and having got some of the Putewatemies privately by themselves, they offered them a Cag of Rum, and said, "We are all Bretheren, we ought to make one Body, and to have one Soul. The French invite us to War against the Five Nations, with design to make us Slaves, and that we should make our selves the Tools to effect it. As soon as they shall have destroyed the Five Nations, they will no longer observe any Measures with us, but use us like those Beasts that they tye to their Plows. Let us leave them to themselves, and they'll never be able to accomplish any thing against the Five Nations.

But the Putewatemies had entertain'd such Notions of the French, as made them Deaf to all the Politicks of the Utawawas.

The French however grew Jealous of these Caballings, and therefore resolv'd to delay their March no longer, and would not stay one day more for the Utawawas, who desired only so much time to Pitch their Canoes, but went away without them.

Mr. Tonti, Commandant among the Chictaghicks, met with another Party of the English of about 30 Men in Lake Ohswego as he marched with the Chictaghicks and Twihtwiks, and other neighbouring Nations to the General Rendevouze. He fell upon the English, Plundered them, and took them Prisoners. The French divided all the Merchandize among the Indians, but kept the Rum to themselves and got all

drunk. The Deonondadie Prisoners, that Conducted the English, joyned with the Mihikander Indians that were among
Mr. Tonti's Indians (who had privately disswaded about 200
of the neighbouring Nations from going along with Tonti) and
endeavoured to perswade all the Indians to fall upon the
French, while they were drunk, and destroy them, saying, *The
French are a Proud, Imperious, Covetous People, that sell their
goods at an extravagant Price: The English are a good
Natured, Honest People, who will furnish you with every thing
at reasonable Rates.* But these arguments were to no purpose,
for these far Indians had entertained extraordinary Notions
of the French Power, and knew nothing of the English.

The French and Putewatemies being gone from Teïo-
dondoraghie, the Utawawas began to be afraid of the French
Resentment, and therefore the better to keep up the colour
they had put on their delays, marched over Land with all
possible expedition, to the general Rendevouz near Oniagara,
where all the French Force, both Christian and Indian was to
meet.

The Five Nations being informed of the French Preparations, laid aside their Designs against the Twihtwies, and
prepared to give the French a warm Reception. Upon this the
Priest at Onnondaga left them, and their Soldiers came to
Albany to provide Ammunition. The Commissioners made
them a Present of a considerable quantity of Powder and Lead,
besides what they purchased. They were under a great deal of
Concern when they took leave of the Commissioners, and said,
"Since we are to expect no other Assistance from our Brethren,
we must recommend our Wives and Children to you, who will
fly to you, if any Misfortune shall happen to us. It may be
we shall never see you more; for we are resolved to behave so
as our Brethren shall have no reason to be ashamed of us."

We must now return to Mr. De Nonville's Army.

Mons. Champigni marched eight or ten Days before the rest
of the Army, with between two and three hundred Canadiens.

As soon as they arriv'd at Cadarackui, they surprized two Villages of the Five Nations, that were settled about eight Leagues from that Place, to prevent their giving any intelligence to their own Nation of the French Preparations, or the State of the French Army, as it was supposed they did in the last Expedition under Mr. De la Barre. These People were surprised when they least expected, and by them from whom they fear'd no harm, because they had settled there at the Invitation and on the Faith of the French. They were carried in cold Blood to the Fort, and tyed to Stakes to be tormented by the French Indians (Christians, as they call them) while they continued singing in their Country manner, and upbraiding the French with their Perfidy and Ungratitude. But the French Policy had no Compassion on these Miserable People, when they were resolved to destroy their whole Nation.

While Mr. De Nonville was at Cadarackui Fort, he had an Account that the Chicktaghiks and Twihtwies waited for the Quatoghies and Utawawas at (*h*) Lake St. Clair, with whom they design'd to March to the general Rendevouz at the Mouth of the Sennekas River. For this Expedition was chiefly design'd against the Sennekas, who had absolutely refused to meet Mr. De la Barre, and were most firmly attached to the English. The Sennekas for this reason were design'd to be made Examples of the French Resentment to all the other Nations of Indians.

The Messenger having assured the General, that it was time to depart, in order to meet the Western Indians, that came to his Assistance, he set out the 23d of June, and sent one part of his Army in Canoes, along the North Shoar, while he with the other part passed along the South, that no accidents of wind might prevent the one or the other reaching within the time appointed at the Place the Indians were to meet him. It happened, by reason of the good weather that both the Parties arrived on the same day, and joyned the Western

(*h*) In the Streights between Ohswego Lake and Quatoghie Lake.

Indians at Irondequat. As soon as the men were put on shoar, they hawled up the Canoes, and began a Fort, where 400 Men were left to guard the Canoes, and the Baggage. Here a young Canadien was shot to death, as a Deserter, for conducting the English into the Lakes, tho' the two Nations were not only at Peace, but their Kings in stricter Friendship than usual. But this Piece of severity is not to be wonder'd at, when the French were resolved to undertake an unjust War, and every thing to put a stop to the English Trade, which now began to extend it self far into the Continent, and would in its consequence ruin theirs. The next day the Army began to march towards the chief Village of the Sennekas, which was only seven Leagues distant, every man carrying ten Biskets for his Provision. The Indian Traders made the Van with part of the Indians, the other part marched in the Rear, while the Regular Troops and Militia compos'd the main Body. The Army marched four Leagues the first day, without discovering any thing. The next day the scouts advanced before the Army, as far as the corn Fields of the Village, without seeing any body, tho' they passed within Pistol shot of 500 Sennekas, that lay on their Bellies, and let them pass and repass, without disturbing them.

On the Report which they made, the French Marched with much haste, but little Order, in hopes to overtake the Women, Children and Old Men; for they no longer doubted of all being fled. But as soon as the French reached the foot of a Hill, about a quarter of a League from the Village, the Sennekas suddenly rais'd the War-shout, with a Discharge of their Fire-Arms. This put the Regular Troops, as well as the Militia into such a Fright, as they marched through the Woods, that the Battalions immediately divided, and run to the Right and Left, and in the Confusion fired upon one another. When the Sennekas perceived their Disorder, they fell in among them Pell-mell, till the French Indians, more used to such Fights, gathered together and Repulsed the

Sennekas. There were (according to the French Accounts) a hundred French-men, ten French Indians, and about fourscore Sennekas kill'd in this Rencounter.

Mr. De Nonvelle was so dis-spirited with the Fright that his Men had been put into, that his Indians could not perswade him to pursue. He halted the remainder of that Day. The next day he Marched on with design to burn the Village, but when he came there, he found the Sennekas had saved him the trouble; for they had laid all in Ashes before they Retired; Two Old Men only were found in the Castle, who were cut into Pieces and boyled to make Soop for the French Allies. The French staid five or six Days to destroy their Corn, and then marched to two other Villages, at two or three Leagues distance. After they had perform'd the like Exploits in those Places they return'd to the Banks of the Lake.

Before the French left the Lakes, they built a Fort of four Bastions at Oniagara, on the South side of the Streights, between Ohswego Lake and Cadarackui Lake, and left a hundred Men, with eight Months Provisions in it. But this Garrison was so closely blockt up by the Five Nations, that they all dy'd of Hunger, except seven or eight, who were accidentally reliev'd by a Party of French Indians.

The Western Indians when they parted from the French General, made their Harrangues, as usual, in which they told him with what Pleasure they saw a Fort so well placed to favour their Designs against the Five Nations, and that they Relied on his never Finishing the War but with the Destruction of the Five Nations, or Forceing them to abandon their Country. He assured them, that he would act with such Vigour that they would soon see the Five Nations driven into the Sea.

He sent a Detachment of Soldiers to Teiodondoraghie, and in his Return to Canada, which was by the North side of the Lake, he left the same Number of Men and Quantity of Provisions at Cadarackui Fort.

The French having got nothing but dry Blows, sent thirteen of the Indians that they surprized at Cadarackui, to France, as Trophies of their Victory, where they were put into the Galleys, as Rebels to their King.

CHAP. VI.

Coll. Dongan's Advice to the Indians. Adario's Enterprize, and Montreal Sacked by the Five Nations.

COLL. Dongan, who always had the Indian Affairs very much at heart, met the Five Nations at Albany as soon as possible after the French Expedition, and spoke to them on the 5th of August, in the following words, *viz.*

Brethren;

"I am very glad to see you here in this House, and am heartily glad that you have sustain'd no greater loss by the French, tho' I believe it was their Intention to destroy you all, if they could have surpriz'd you in your Castles.

"As soon as I heard of their design to War with you, I gave you Notice, and came up hither my self, that I might be ready to give all the Assistance and Advice that so short a time would allow me.

"I am now about sending a Gentleman to England, to the King, my Master, to let him know, that the French have invaded his Territories on this side the great Lake, and War'd upon the Brethren, his Subjects. I would therefore willingly know, whether the Brethren have given the Governor of Canada any Provocation or not; and if they have, how, and in what manner, because I am oblig'd to give a true account of this matter. This business may cause a War between the King of England and the French King, both in Europe and here, and therefore I must know the Truth.

"I know the Governor of Canada dare not enter into the great King of England's Territories, in a Hostile manner, without Provocation, if he thought the Brethren were the King of England's Subjects; But you having two or three years ago, made a Covenant Chain with the French, contrary to my Command, (which I knew could not hold long) being void of it self among the Christians; for as much as Subjects (as you are) ought not to treat with any Foreign Nation, it not lying in your Power, have brought this Trouble upon your selves, and, as I believe, is the only reason of their falling upon you at this time.

"Brethren, I took it very ill, that after you had put your selves into the Number of the great King of England's Subjects, that you should ever offer to make Peace or War without my consent. You know that we can live without you, but you cannot live without us. You never found that I told you a Lie, and I did offer you Assistance as you wanted, provided that you would be advised by me; for I know the French better than any of you do.

"Now since there is a War begun upon you by the Governor of Canada, I hope without any Provocation by you given, I desire and command you, that you hearken to no Treaty but by my Advice, which if you follow, you shall have the Benefit of the great Chain of Friendship between the great King of England and the French King, which came out of England the other day, and which I have sent to Canada by Anthony Le Junard. In the mean time I will give you such Advice as will be for your good, and will supply you with such Necessarys as you will have need of.

"*First,* My Advice is, that as many Prisoners of the French, as you shall take, that you draw not their Blood, but bring them home and keep them to Exchange for your People, which they have Prisoners already, or may take hereafter.

"*2dly,* That if it be Possible, that you can order it so, I would have you take one or two of your wisest Sachems, and one or two chief Captains of each Nation, to be a Council to manage all Affairs of the War. They to give Orders to the rest of the Officers what they are to do, that your designs may be kept Private, for after it comes among so many People, it is Blazed abroad, and your designs are often frustrated. And those chief Men to keep a Correspondence with me, by a Trusty Messenger.

"3*dly,* Now the Great matter under Consideration with the Brethren, is, how to strengthen themselves, and weaken your Enemy. My Opinion is, that the Brethren should send Messengers to the Utawawas, Twihtwichs, and the farther Indians, and to send back likewise some of the Prisoners of these Nations, if any you have left, to bury the Hatchet, and to make a Covenant Chain, that they may put away all the French that are among them, and that you will open a Path for them this way, They being the King of England's Subjects likewise, only the French have been admitted to Trade with them, for all that the French have in Canada, they had it of the Great King of England, that by that Means they may come hither freely where they may have every thing Cheaper than among the French. That you and they may joyn together against the French, and make so firm a League that whoever is an Enemy to one, must be to both.

"4*thly,* Another thing of Concern is, that you ought to do what you can to open a Path for all the North Indians and Mahikanders that are among the Utawawas and farther Nations: I will endeavour to do the same, to bring them home; for they not daring to return home your way, the French keep them there on purpose to joyn with the farther Nations against you, for your Destruction; for you know, that one of them is worse than six of the others. Therefore all means must be used to bring them Home, and use them kindly as they pass through your Country.

"5*thly,* My Advice further is, That Messengers go in behalf of all the Five Nations, to the Christian Indians at Canada, to perswade them to come Home to their Native Country, and to promise them all Protection. This will be another great means to weaken your Enemy; but if they will not be advised, you know what to do with them.

"6*thly,* I think it very necessary for the Brethrens Security and Assistance, and to the endamaging the French, to build a Fort upon the Lake, where I may keep Stores and Provisions in case of necessity; and therefore I would have the Brethren let me know what Place will be most convenient for it.

"7*thly,* I would not have the Brethren keep their Corn in their Castles, as I hear the Onnondagas do, but to bury it a great way in the Woods, where few People may know where it is, for fear of such an Accident as has happen'd to the Sennekas.

"8*thly,* I have given my Advice in your General Assembly by Mr. Dirk Wessels and Akus the Interpreter, how you are to manage your Partys, and how necessary it is to get Prisoners, to exchange for your own Men that are Prisoners with the French. And I am glad to hear that the Brethren are so United, as Mr. Dirk Wessels tells me you are, and that there are no Rotten Members nor French Spyes among you.

"9*thly,* The Brethren may remember my Advice which I sent you this Spring, Not to go to Cadarackui; if you had, they would have serv'd you as they did your People who came from Hunting thither; for I told you then, that I knew the French better than you did.

"10*thly.* There was no Advice or Proposition that I made to the Brethren, all the time that the Priest liv'd at Onondaga, but what he wrote to Canada, as I found by one of his Letters, which he gave to an Indian to carry to Canada, but was brought hither. Therefore I desire the Brethren not to receive him or any French Priests any more, having sent for English Priests, with whom you may be supply'd to your Content.

"11. I would have the Brethren look out sharp for fear of being surprised. I believe all the Strength of the French will be at their Frontier Places, *viz.* at Cadarackui and Oniagara, where they build a Fort now, and at Trois Rivieres, Montreal and Chambly.

"12. Let me put you in mind again, not to make any Treatys without my Means, which will be more Advantagious for you, than your doing it by your selves, for then you will be look'd upon as the King of England's Subjects. And let me know, from time to time, every thing that is done.

"Thus far I have spoken to you relating to the War."

Then he chid them for their Breach of Faith with Virginia. He told them, that he was inform'd that last Spring they had kill'd a fine Gentleman, with some others, and that a Party of the Oneydoes was now there at the head of James River, with intention to destroy all the Indians there-about. They had taken six Prisoners, whom he order'd them to bring to him, to be Restored; and that for the future they should desist from doing any Injury to the People of Virginia or their Indians, otherwise all the English would unite to destroy them. But at the same time he free'd the Sennekas from any blame, and commended them as a brave and honest People, who never had done any thing contrary to his Orders, except in making that unlucky Peace with the French three years ago.

Lastly, He recommended to them, Not to suffer their People to be Drunk, during the War: A Soldier thereby (he said) looses his Reputation, because of the Advantages it will give the Enemy over him.

This honest Gentleman earnestly pursued the Interest of his Country; but, it seems, his Measures were not agreeable to those his Master had taken with the French King; for he had Orders to procure a Peace for the French, and was soon after this Removed from his Government. Indeed such an Active, as well as Prudent Governor of New-York, could not be acceptable to the French, who had the Universal Monarchy in view, in America as well as in Europe.

Coll. Dongan's Message to Mr. De Nonville at a time when the Crowns of England and France had so lately entred into a strict Friendship, had, no doubt, some Influence on the French Governor. But the little Success he had in his Expensive and Dangerous Expedition, together with the Obstruction that the French Trade met with from the War, inclin'd him more effectually to Proposals of Peace, which Coll. Dongan was forced to make, and the Five Nations to yield to: For notwithstanding Coll. Dongan's Advice to them, as above related, he by his Masters Orders (who was entirely devoted to Bigotry and the French Interest) obliged the Five Nations to agree to a Cessation of Arms, and to deliver up their Prisoners without any Conditions, in order to obtain a Peace on such Terms as the French should agree to. And that no Accident might prevent this, Mr. De Nonville sent his Orders to all his Officers in the Indian Countrys to observe a Cessation of Arms till the Ambassadors of the Five Nations should meet him at Montreal, as they had given him reason to expect in a little time, to conclude the Peace in the usual Form.

In the mean time, Adario, the chief of the Deonondadies, finding that his Nation was become suspected by the French, since the time they had shown so much Inclination to the English when they attempted to Trade at Missilimakinak, Resolved by some brave Action against the Five Nations to recover the good Graces of the French.

For this Purpose he Marched from Missilimakinak at the head of a hundred Men; and that he might act with more Security, he took Cadarackui Fort in his way for Intelligence: The Commandant informed him, that Mr. De Nonville was in hopes of concluding a Peace with the Five Nations, and expected their Embassadors in eight or ten days at Montreal for that purpose, and therefore desired him to return to Missilimakinak without attempting any thing that might Obstruct so good a Design.

The Indian being surprized with this News, was under great Concern for his Nation, which he was afraid would be sacrificed to the French Resentment or Interest, but dissembled his Concern before the French Officer. He went from Cadarackui, not to return home as the Commandant thought, but to wait for the Ambassadors of the 5 Nations near one of the Falls of Cadarackui River, by which he knew they must pass.

He did not lurk there above four or five days before the un-happy Deputies came guarded by forty young Soldiers, who were all surprised & kill'd or taken Prisoners. As soon as the Prisoners were all secured, the cunning Deonondadie told them "That he having been enformed by the Governor of Canada, That Fifty Warriors of their Nation were to pass this way about this time, he had secured this Pass, not doubting of intercepting them."

The Ambassadors being much surpris'd with the French Perfidy, told Adario the Design of their Journey, who, the better to play his part, seem'd to grow Mad and Furious, de-claiming against Mr. De Nonville, and said, *He would, some Time or other be Revenged of him for making a Tool of him to commit such horrid Treachery.* Then looking stedfastly on the Prisoners (among whom Dekanesora was the Principal Ambassador) Adario said to them, *Go my Brethren, I Unty your Bonds, and send you Home again, tho' our Nations be at War; The French Governor has made me commit so black an Action, that I shall never be easy after it till your Five Nations shall have taken full Vengeance.*

This was sufficient to perswade the Ambassadors of the Truth of what he said, who assured him, That he and his Na-tion might make their Peace when they pleased. Adario lost only one Man on this occasion, and would keep a Satana Slave, (adopted into the Five Nations) to fill up his place. Then he gave Arms, Powder and Ball to the rest of the Prisoners, to enable them to Return.

The Ambassadors were chiefly if not all, Onnondagas and Oneydoes, who had been long under the influence of the French Priests, and still retain'd an Affection to them; but this Adventure throughly changed their thoughts, and irri-tated them so heartily against the French, that all the Five Nations from this time prosecuted the War unanimously.

Adario deliver'd the Slave (his Prisoner) to the French at Missilimakinak, who to keep up the Enmity between the Deonondadies and the Five Nations, order'd him to be shot to Death. As they carried him out, he related the whole of

the Action, but the French thinking that he had only contrived it to save his Life, had no regard to it, till the fatal
Consequences call'd his Dying Words to their Remembrance,
with sorrowful Reflections.

The same Day that the Satana was shot, Adario call'd one of
the Five Nations, who had been long a Prisoner, to be an
Eye-witness of his Country-mans Death, then bid him make
his Escape to his own Country, to give an Account of the
French Cruelty, from which it was not in his Power to save a
Prisoner he himself had taken.

This heighten'd the Rage of the Five Nations, so that Mr.
De Nonville's sending to disown Adario in this Action, had
no effect upon them: Their Breasts admitted of no thought
but that of Revenge. It was not long before the French felt
the Bloody effects of this cruel Passion; for 1200 Men of the
Five Nations invaded the island of Montreal when the French
had no suspicion of any such Attempt, while Mr. De Nonville
and his Lady were in that Town. They Landed on the south
side of the Island at La Chine, on the 26th of July, 1688.
where they burnt and sacked all the Plantations, and made a
terrible Massacre of Men, Women and Children. The French
were under apprehension of the Town's being attacked, for
which reason they durst not send out any considerable Party
to the Relief of the Country, till the Indians had blocked up
two Forts, then Mr. De Nonville sent out a hundred Soldiers
and fifty Indians to try to bring off the men, The French of
this Party were all either taken or cut to pieces, except one
Soldier and the Commanding Officer, who was carried off by
twelve Indians that made their escape, after he had his Thigh
broke. There was above a Thousand of the French kill'd at
this time, and Twenty six were carried away Prisoners, the
greatest part of which were burnt alive. The Five Nations only
lost three Men in this Expedition, that got Drunk, and were
left behind. This, however, did not satiate their Thirst after
Blood; for in October following they destroy'd likewise all
the lower part of the Island, and carried away many Prisoners.

The Consequences of these Expeditions were very dismal

to the French, for they were forced to burn their two Barks which they had on Cadarackui Lake, and to abandon their Fort there. They design'd to have blown up their Works when they left that place, and for that end left a lighted Match where the Powder lay, but were in such a Fright, that they durst not stay to see what effect it had. They went down Cadarackui River, in seven Birch Canoes, and for greater Security travel'd in the Night. One of the Canoes with all the men in it was lost by their Precipitation, as they passed one of the Falls of that River. The Five Nations hearing that the French had deserted Cadarackui Fort, 50 Indians went and took Possession of it, who found the Match the French had left, which had gone out, and 28 Barrils of Powder in the same place, together with several other Stores.

The News of the Success the Five Nations had over the French, soon spread itself among all the Indians, and put the French Affairs every where into terrible Disorder.

The Utawawas had always shown an Inclination to the English, and they therefore immediately sent openly four Sachems with three Prisoners of the Sennekas that they had, to assure them, That they would forever Renounce all Friendship with the French, and promised to Restore the rest of the Prisoners. They also included seven Nations that liv'd near Missilimakinak, in this Peace.

This put the French commandant there under the greatest Difficulty to maintain his Post; but there was no Choice, he must stand his Ground; for the Five Nations had cut off all hopes of Retiring.

The Nepeciriniens and Kikabous, of all their Numerous Allies, only remain'd firm to the French, every one of the others endeavour'd to gain the Friendship of the 5 Nations, and would certainly have done it, by Massacreing all the French among them, if the Sieur Perot had not with wonderful Sagacity and imminent Hazard to his own Person diverted them, for which Canada cannot do too much Honour to that Gentlemans Memory.

Canada was now in a most Miserable Condition; for while

the greatest Number of their Men had been employ'd in the Expeditions against the Five Nations, and in Trading among the far Nations, and making New Discoveries and Settlements, Tillage and Husbandry had been neglected; now they lost several Thousands of their Inhabitants by the continual Incursions of small Parties, so that none durst hazard themselves out of the Fortified Places. Indeed, it is not easie to conceive what Distress the French were then under; for tho' they were almost every where starving, they could not Plant nor Sow, or go from one Village to another for Relief, but with imminent Danger of having their Scalps carried away by the Sculking Indians. At last the whole Country being laid Waste, Famine began to rage, and was like to have put a Miserable End to that Colony.

If the Indians had understood the method of attacking Forts, nothing could have preserved the French from an entire Destruction at this time. For whoever considers the state of the Indian Affairs during this Period, How the Five Nations were divided in their Sentiements and Measures; The Onnondagas, Cayugas, and Oneydoes, under the Influence of the French Jesuits, were diverted from prosecuting the War with Canada, by the Jesuits cunningly spiriting up those three Nations against the Virginia Indians, and perswading them to send out their Parties that way: The Sennekas had a War at the same time upon their hands with three numerous Indian Nations, the Utawawas, Chicktaghicks and Twihtwies: And the Measures the English observed with the French all King James's Reign, gave the Indians rather grounds of Jealousy than Assistance. I say, whoever considers all these things, and what the Five Nations did actually perform under all these Disadvantages against the French, will hardly doubt that the Five Nations by themselves were at that time an over Match for the French of CANADA.

The End of the First Part.

Part II.

The History of the Five Indian Nations . . . from the Time of the Revolution to the Peace of Reswick.

The Preface to the Second Part.

THE former Part of this History was written at New-York in the Year 1727, on Occasion of a Dispute which then happened, between the Government of New-York and some Merchants. The French of Canada had the whole Fur Trade with the Western Indians in their Hands, and were supplied with their woollen Goods from New-York. Mr. Burnet, who took more Pains to be informed of the Interest of the People he was set over, and of making them useful to their Mother Country, than Plantation Governors usually do, took the Trouble of perusing all the Registers of the Indian Affairs on this Occasion. He from thence conceived of what Consequence the Fur Trade with the Western Indians was of to Great-Britain; that as the English had the Fur Trade to Hudson's Bay given up to them, by the Treaty of Utrecht, so, by the Advantages which the Province of New-York has in its Situation, they might be able to draw the whole Fur Trade in the other Parts of America to themselves, and thereby the English engross that Trade, and the Manufactories depending on it.

For this Purpose he thought it necessary to put a Stop to the Trade between New-York and Canada, by which the French supplied themselves with the most valuable and necessary Commodities for the Indian Market, and to set the Inhabitants of this Province on trading directly with the Indians. Besides the Consideration of Profit and Gain, he considered what Influence this Trade had on the numerous Nations of Indians living on the vast Continent of North-America, and who surround the British Colonies; of what Advantage it might be of, if they were influenced by the English in Case of a War with France; and how prejudicial, on the other Hand, if they were directed by French Counsels.

The Legislature of New-York was soon convinced of the Justness of his Reasoning, and passed an Act, prohibiting the Trade to Canada, and for encouraging the Trade directly with the Indians. They were likewise at the Charge of building a fortified trading House at Oswego, on Cadarackui Lake, and have ever since maintained a Garison there. As this Act did in its Consequence take a large Profit from one or two considerable Merchants, who had the Trade to Canada intirely in their Hands, they endeavoured to raise a Clamour against it in the Province, and presented likewise Petitions to the King, in Order to get the Act repealed. Upon this Occasion Mr. Burnet gave me the Perusal of the Publick Register of Indian Affairs, and it was thought the Publication of the History of the Five Nations might be of Use at that Time.

I shall only add, that Mr. Burnet's Scheme has had its desired Effect: The English have gained the Trade which the French, before that, had with the Indians to the Westward of New-York; and whereas, before that Time, a very inconsiderable Number of Men were employed in the Indian Trade Abroad, now above three hundred Men are employed at the Trading House at Oswego alone; and the Indian Trade has since that Time yearly increased so far, that several Indian Nations come now every Summer to trade there, whose Names were not so much as known by the English before.

This History, from New-York, soon went to England, and I have been informed, that a Publication, with a Continuance of that Work, would be acceptable there. I have the more chearfully complied with this Notice, because of the War threatened from France, believing that a Publication of this Kind may be useful, whether the present Inquietudes between the two Nations end in a War or in a Treaty. The French have encouraged several Publications of this Sort at

Paris, and certainly such may be more useful in a British Government, where the People have so great a Share in it, than it can be in a French Government, intirely directed by the Will of their Prince.

I now continue this History to the Peace of Reswick, and if I find this acceptable, and that a farther Continuation of it be desired, I shall, if my Life and Health be preserved, carry it down farther; but as I have too much Reason to doubt my own Ability, to give that Pleasure and Satisfaction which the Publick may expect in Things thus submitted to their View, I think it not justifiable to trouble them with too much at once.

CHAP. I.

The State of Affairs in New-York and Canada, at the Time of the Revolution in Great-Britain.

WE left the Five Nations triumphing over the French in Canada, and they almost reduced to Despair. The Revolution, which happened at this Time in England, seemed to be a favourable Conjunction for the Five Nations; the English Colonies, by the War at that Time declared against France, becoming Parties in their Quarrel: For one will be ready to think, that the Five Nations being by themselves too powerful for the French, as appears by the preceding Chapter, when these were assisted by the Utawawas, Quatoghies, Twihtwies, Chictaghicks, Putewatemies, and all the Western Indian Nations, and when the English stood neuter; now certainly, when not only all these Indian Nations had made Peace with the Five Nations, but the English joined with them in the War, the French would not be able to stand one Campaign.

But we shall find what a Turn Affairs took, contrary to all reasonable Expectations, from the general Appearance of Things, and of what Importance a resolute wise Governor is to the well-being of a People, and how prejudicial Divisions and Parties are. For this Reason, it will be necessary to take a View of the Publick Affairs in the Province of New-York, and in Canada, at that Time, in order to understand the true Causes of the Alterations, which afterwards happened in Favour of the French.

The Revolution occasioned as great Divisions and Parties

in the Province of New-York, in Proportion to the Number of People, as it did in Britain, if not greater. The Governor and all the Officers either fled or absconded; the Gentlemen of the King's Council, and some of the most considerable or richest People, either out of Love, or what they thought Duty, to King James, or rather from an Opinion they had that the Prince of Orange could not succeed, refused to join in the declaration the People made in favour of that Prince, and suffered the Administration to fall into different Hands, who were more zealous for the Protestant Interest, and who were joined by the far greatest Number of the Inhabitants. After the Revolution was established, they that had appeared so warmly for it, thought that they deserved best of the Government, and expected to be continued in the Publick Offices; the others were zealous to recover the Authority they had lost, and used the most persuasive Means with the Governors for that Purpose, while the former trusted to their Merit. This begat great Animosities, which continued many Years. Each Party, as they were at different Times favoured by several Governors, opposed all the Measures taken by the other, while each of them were by Turns in Credit with the People or the Governor, and sometimes even prosecuted each other to Death. The publick Measures were by these Means perpetually fluctuating, and often one Day contradictory to what they were the Day before. The succeeding Governors, finding their private Account in favouring sometimes the one Party, and at other Times the other, kept up the Animosities all King William's Reign, though very much to the publick Prejudice; for each Party was this while so eager in resenting private Injuries, that they intirely neglected the publick Good.

The Constitution of Government in the English Plantations, where the Governors have no Salary, but what they can attain with the Consent of the Assemblies or Representatives of the People, gave Occasion to imprudent Governors to fall upon these Expedients, as they sometimes call them, for getting of Money. And a prevailing Faction, knowing for what

Purpose the Governments in America were chiefly desired by the English Gentlemen, used this great Privilege to tempt a Governor to be the Head of a Party, when he ought to have been the Head of the Government. Indeed New-York has had the Misfortune, too frequently, to be under such as could not keep their Passion for Money secret, though none found it so profitable a Government, as they did who followed strictly the true Maxims of governing, without making Money the only Rule of their Actions.

The frequent Changes of Governors were likewise prejudicial to the publick Affairs. Colonel Slaughter, the first Governor after the Revolution, happened to die soon after his Arrival, when steady, as well as resolute Measures, were most necessary. But some think, that the Occasion of all the Misfortunes lay in the Want of Care in the Choice of Governors, when the Affairs of America wanted able Hands to manage them; they think that the Ministry had the saving of Money chiefly in View, when, to gratify some small Services, they gave Employments in America to those that were not capable of much meaner Offices at Home. The Opinion the People had of Colonel Slaughter's Capacity gave ground to these Surmises; but, if it was so, it happened to be very ill saved Money; for the Mismanagements in this Country occasioned far greater Expence to the Crown afterwards, than would have bought such Gentlemen handsome Estates, besides the great Losses they occasioned to the Subjects.

The greatest Number of the Inhabitants of the Province of New-York being Dutch, still retained an Affection to their Mother Country, and by their Aversion to the English weakened the Administration. The common People of Albany, who are all Dutch, could not forbear giving the Indians some ill Impressions of the English; for the Mohawks, in one of their publick Speeches, expressed themselves thus: "We hear a Dutch Prince reigns now in England, why do you suffer the English Soldiers to remain in the Fort? put all the English out of the Town. When the Dutch held this Country long ago, we lay in their Houses; but the English have always made us lie without Doors." It is true, that the Plantations were first settled by the meanest People of every Nation, and such as had the least Sense of any Honour. The Dutch first Settlers, many of them I may say, had none of the Virtues of their Countrymen, except their Industry in getting Money, and they sacrificed every Thing, other People think honourable or most sacred, to their Gain: But I do not think it proper to give particular Instances of this.

The People of New-England were engaged in a bloody War at this Time with the Owenagungas, Ouragies, and Ponacoks, the Indians that lie between them and the French Settlements. The Scahkooks were originally Part of these Indians. They left their Country about the Year 1672, and settled above Albany, on the Branch of Hudson's River that runs towards Canada. The People of New-England were jealous of the Scahkook Indians, that they remembering the Old Difference they had with the People of New England, and the Relation they bore to the Eastern Indians, did countenance and assist these Indians in the War against New England. They had Reason for these Jealousies, for the Scahkook Indians received privately some Owenagunga Messengers, and kept their coming among them secret from the People of Albany; and some Scahkooks had gone privately to the Owenagungas. They were afraid likewise, that the Mohawks might have some Inclination to favour those Indians, because some of the Eastern Indians had fled to the Mohawks, and were kindly received by them, and lived among them.

Notwithstanding all these Failures of good Policy, in the Government of New-York, the French had not gained so great Advantages, if they had not carefully observed a different Conduct, which it is now necessary to consider.

Canada was at this Time in a very distressed Condition, the Country and out Plantations burnt and destroyed, their Trade intirely at a stand, great Numbers of their People slain, and the remainder in danger of perishing by Famine, as well as

by the Sword of inveterate cruel Enemies. When such Misfortunes happen to a Country, under any Administration,
though in Truth the Conduct of Affairs be not to be blamed,
it is often prudent to change the Ministers; for the common
People never fail to blame them, notwithstanding their having acted with the greatest Wisdom, and therefore cannot so
soon recover their Spirits, that are sunk by Misfortunes, as by
putting their Affairs into different Hands.

For these Reasons, it is probable, the French King recalled
Mr. de Nonville, but rewarded him for his Services, by an
honourable Employment in the Houshold. The Count de
Frontenac was sent in his Place. This Gentleman had been
formerly Governor of that Country, and was perfectly acquainted with its Interest; of a Temper of Mind fitted to such
desperate Times, of undaunted Courage, and indefatigable,
though in the sixty-eighth Year of his Age. The Count de
Frontenac arrived the second of October 1689. The Country
immediately received new Life by the Arrival of a Person,
of whose Courage and Conduct every one had entertained a
high Opinion. Care was taken to increase this Impression on
the Minds of the People, by making publick Rejoicings with as
much Noise as possible. He wisely improved this new Life, by
immediately entering upon Action, without suffering their
Hopes to grow cold. He staid no longer at Quebeck, than was
necessary to be informed of the present State of Affairs, and
in four or five Days after his Arrival set out in a Canoe for
Montreal, where his Presence was most necessary; and the
Winter was already so far advanced, that the Ice made it im-
practicable to go in a larger Vessel. By this the old Gentleman
increased the Opinion and Hopes the People entertained of
him, that, without staying to refresh himself after a fatiguing
Sea-Voyage, he would immediately undertake another, that
required all the Vigour and Heat of Youth to withstand the
Inclemencies of the Climate and Season, and the Difficulty of
such a Passage.

When the Count de Frontenac came to Montreal, he in-

creased the Admiration the People had of his Vigour and
Zeal, by pretending to go to visit Cadarackui Fort, now aban-
doned, which he had built in the Time he was formerly Governor. The Clergy and People of Montreal came jointly with
stretched out Arms, representing the Danger of such an Attempt, and the Difficulties and Hardships that would neces-
sarily attend it, praying him not to expose a Life that was so
necessary for their Safety. He, with seeming Reluctance,
yielded to their Intreaties; I say with seeming Reluctance, for
it was inconsistent with his Prudence really to have such a
Design. This Shew of the Governor's offering to go in Person, animated some of the Gentlemen of the Country, who
voluntarily went in the Winter, with one Hundred Indian
Traders, to visit that Fort; and finding it in better Condition
than they expected, by the Report of those who had aban-
doned it, they staid there, and made some small Reparations
in the Walls, which the Indians had thrown down.

The Count de Frontenac brought back with him Tawerahet, a Capiga Sachem, one of the thirteen Prisoners that Mr.
de Nonville took at Cadarackui, and sent to France. He was
in Hopes this Indian would be useful in procuring a Treaty
of Peace with the Five Nations, for they had an extraordinary
Opinion of Tawerahet; and the French had found, by sad
Experience, that they could not be Gainers by continuing the
War: For this Purpose the Count used Tawerahet with much
Kindness, during his Voyage, and, after he arrived at Quebeck, lodged him in the Castle under his own Roof, and took
such Pains with this Sachem, that he forgot all the ill Usage
he had formerly received.

The French had the more Reason to desire a Peace with the
Five Nations, because they knew, that they would now certainly have the English Colonies likewise upon them; and if
the Five Nations had been able to do so much Mischief by
themselves alone, they were much more to be feared, when
they would be assisted, in all Probability, with the Force
and Interest of the English Colonies.

Four Indians of less Note, who were brought back along with Tawerahet, were immediately dispatched, in this Sachem's Name, to the Five Nations, to inform them of his Return, and of the kind Usage they had received from the Count de Frontenac; and to press them to send some to visit their old Friend, who had been so kind to them when he was formerly Governor of Canada, and who still retained an Affection to the Five Nations; as appeared by the Kindness Tawerahet and they had received from him. This was the only Method left to the French of making Proposals of Peace, which it was their Interest by all Means to procure.

The Governor of Canada, as I said, conceived that there was no Way so proper to keep up the Spirits of the People, who had got new Life by his Arrival, as by putting them upon Action; and indeed their present miserable Condition made them forward enough, to undertake the most desperate Enterprize, when the frequent Incursions of the Indians made it as dangerous to be at Home, as to attack the Enemy Abroad.

For this Purpose he sent out three Parties in the Winter; one was designed against New-York, the other against Connecticut, and the last against New-England.

The Five Nations followed Colonel Dungan's Advice, in endeavouring to bring off the Western Indians from the French, and had all the Success that could be expected, before Mr. de Frontenac arrived.

They were overjoyed when they heard, that the English had entered into War with the French, and came several Times to Albany to know the Certainty of it, while it was only rumoured about. The People of Albany desired them to secure any of the praying Indians that should come from Canada, if they found that they were still ruled by the Priests; but to encourage them, if they came with a Design to return to their own Country.

The Senekas, Cayugas, Onondagas, and Oneydoes, the twenty seventh of June 1689, before any Governor arrived, renewed the old Covenant (as they said) which was first made many Years ago with one Tagues, who came with a Ship into their River. "Then we first became Brethren, said they, and continued so till last fall, that Sir Edmond Andross came and made a new Chain, by calling us Children; but let us stick to the old Chain, which has continued from the first Time it was made, by which we became Brethren, and have ever since always behaved as such. Virginia, Maryland, and New-England, have been taken into this silver Chain, with which our Friendship is locked fast. We are now come to make the Chain clear and bright. Here they gave two Bevers."

King James, a little before his Abdication, sent over Sir Edmond Andross with arbitrary Powers, and he, in Imitation of the French, changed the Stile of speaking to the Indians, of which they were very sensible.

They discovered a great Concern for their People that were carried to Canada; they long hoped (they said) that the King of England would have been powerful enough to deliver them, but now they began to lose all Hopes of them.

CHAP. II.

A Treaty between the Agents of Massachuset's Bay, New-Plymouth, and Connecticut, and the Sachems of the Five Nations, at Albany, in the Year 1689.

ABOUT the Beginning of September 1689, Colonel John Pynchon, Major John Savage, and Captain Jonathan Bull, Agents for the Colonies of Massachuset's Bay, New-Plymouth, and Connecticut, arrived at Albany, to renew the Friendship with the Five Nations, and to engage them against the Eastern Indians, who made War on the English of those Colonies, and were supported by the French.

The Five Nations had received four Messengers from the Eastern Indians, which gave the People of New-England some Apprehensions, and they were therefore desirous to know what Reception these Messengers had met with.

The Five Nations answered by Tahajadoris, a Mohawk Sachem, on the twenty fourth of September. He made a long Oration, repeating all that the Agent from New-England had said, the Day before, and desired them to be attentive to the Answer now to be made to them. They commonly repeat over all that has been said to them, before they return any Answer, and one may be surprized at the Exactness of these Repetitions. They take the following Method to assist their Memories: The Sachem, who presides at these Conferences, has a Bundle of small Sticks in his Hand; as soon as the Speaker has finished any one Article of his Speech, this Sachem gives a Stick to another Sachem, who is particularly to remember that Article; and so when another Article is finished, he gives a Stick to another to take Care of that other, and so on. In like Manner when the Speaker answers, each of these has the particular Care of the Answer resolved on to each Article, and prompts the Orator, when his Memory fails him, in the Article committed to his Charge. Tahajadoris addressing himself to the Agents, said:

"Brethren,

"You are welcome to this House, which is appointed for our Treaties and publick Business with the Christians; we thank you for renewing the Covenant-chain. It is now no longer of Iron and subject to Rust, as formerly, but of pure Silver, and includes in it all the King's Subjects, from the Senekas Country eastward, as far as any of the great King's Subjects live, and southward, from New-England to Virginia. Here he gave a Bever.

"We are glad to hear of the good Success our great King has had over the French by Sea, in taking and sinking so many of their Men of War. You tell us in your Proposals that we are one People, let us then go Hand in Hand together, to ruin and destroy the French our common Enemy. Gives a Bever.

"The Covenant-chain between us is ancient (as you tell us) and of long standing, and it has been kept inviolably by us. When you had Wars some time ago with the Indians, you desired us to help you; we did it readily, and to the Purpose; for we pursued them closely, by which we prevented the Effusion of much of your Blood. This was a certain Sign that we loved truly and sincerely, and from our Hearts. Gives a Belt.

"You advise us to pursue our Enemies, the French, vigorously; this we assure you we are resolved to do to the utmost of our Power: But since the French are your Enemies likewise, we desire our Brethren of the three Colonies to send us an hundred Men for the Security of this Place, which is ill provided, in Case of an Attack from the French; the Christians have Victuals enough for their Entertainment. Gives one Belt.

"We patiently bore many Injuries from the French, from one Year to another, before we took up the Axe against them. Our Patience made the Governor of Canada think, that we were afraid of him, and durst not resent the Injuries we had so long suffered; but now he is undeceived. We assure you, that we are resolved never to drop the Axe, the French never shall see our Faces in Peace, we shall never be reconciled as long as one Frenchman is alive. We shall never make Peace, though our Nation should be ruined by it, and every one of us cut in Pieces. Our Brethren of the three Colonies may depend on this. Gives a Bever.

"As to what you told us of the Owenagungas and Uragees, we answer: That we were never so proud and haughty, as to begin a War without just Provocation. You tell us that they are treacherous Rogues, we believe it, and that they will undoubtedly assist the French. If they shall do this, or shall join with any of our Enemies, either French or Indians, then we will kill and destroy them. Gives a Bever."

Then the Mohawks offered five of their Men, to guard the Agents Home against any of their Indian Enemies, who they were afraid might be laying in wait for the Agents, and gave a Belt.

Afterwards the Speaker continued his Speech, and said: "We have spoke what we had to say of the War, we now come to the Affairs of Peace: We promise to preserve the Chain inviolably, and wish that the Sun may always shine in Peace over all our Heads that are comprehended in this Chain. We give two Belts, one for the Sun, the other for its Beams.

"We make fast the Roots of the Tree of Peace and Tranquillity, which is planted in this Place. Its Roots extend as far as the utmost of your Colonies; if the French should come to shake this Tree, we would feel it by the Motion of its Roots, which extend into our Country: But we trust it will not be in the Governor of Canada's Power to shake this Tree, which has been so firmly and so long planted with us. Gives two Bevers."

Lastly, He desired the Magistrates of Albany to remember what he had said, and gave them a Bever.

But the Agents perceiving, that they had not answered any Thing about the Owenagunga Messengers, and had answered indistinctly about the War with the Eastern Indians, desired them to explain themselves fully on these two Points, about which the Agents were chiefly concerned.

The Five Nations answered:

"We cannot declare War against the Eastern Indians, for they have done us no Harm: Nevertheless our Brethren of New-England may be assured, that we will live and die in Friendship with them. When we took up the Axe against the French and their Confederates, we did it to revenge the Injuries they had done us; we did not make War with them at the Persuasions of our Brethren here; for we did not so much as acquaint them with our Intention, till fourteen Days after our Army had begun their March."

After the Company had separated, the Sachems sent to the New-England Agents, desiring to speak with them in private; which being granted, the Speaker said, we have something to tell you, which was not proper to be spoken openly, for some of our People have an Affection to the Owenagungas; and we were afraid, that they would discover or hinder our Designs.

Now we assure our Brethren, that we are resolved to look on your Enemies as ours, and that we will first fall on the Owaragees; * and then on the Owenagungas, and lastly on the French; and that you may be convinced of our Intention, we design to send five of our young Men along with our Brethren to New-England, to guard them, who have Orders to view the Country of the Owaragees, to discover in what Manner it can be attacked with the most Advantage. This we always do before we make an Attempt on our Enemies. In a Word, Brethren, your War is our War, for we will live and dye with you.

But it is to be observed, that they confirmed nothing relating to these Indians, by giving Belts.

It is probable, that the Sachems acted with some Art on this Occasion, for they really had favourable Inclinations towards the Owenagungas; and they had Reason not to increase the Number of their Enemies, by making War on the Eastern Indians, who avoided doing them any Injury. The People of Albany likewise have always been averse to engage our Indians in a War with the Eastern Indians, lest it should change the Seat of the War, and bring it to their own Doors.

On the 25th the Magistrates of Albany had a private Conference with the Sachems of the Five Nations, and desired to know their Resolutions as to the War with Canada, and the Measures they resolved to follow. In this Conference the Indians saw that the People of Albany were so much afraid of

* Called by the People of New-England Panocok Indians.

the French, that their Spirits were sunk under the Apprehensions of the approaching War; and for this Reason made the following Answer.

"We have a hundred and forty Men out-skulking about Canada; it is impossible for the French to attempt any Thing, without being discovered and harassed by these Parties: If the French shall attempt any Thing this Way, all the Five Nations will come to your Assistance, for our Brethren and we are but one, and we will live and dye together. We have desired a hundred Men of our Brethren of Boston to assist us here, because this Place is most exposed; but if the Governor of Canada is so strong, as to overcome us all united together, then he must be our Master, and is not to be resisted; but we have Confidence in a good and just Cause; for the great God of Heaven knows how deceitfully the French have dealt with us, their Arms can have no Success. The Great God hath sent us Signs in the Sky to confirm this. We have heard uncommon Noise in the Heavens, and have seen Heads fall down upon Earth, which we look upon as a certain Presage of the Destruction of the French: Take Courage! On this they all immediately joined in singing and crying out, Courage! Courage!"

CHAP. III.

An Account of a general Council of the Five Nations at Onondaga, to consider the Count De Frontenac's Message.

ON the 27th of December 1689, two Indians came to Albany, being sent by the Onondaga and Oneydo Sachems, with seven Hands of Wampum from each Nation, to tell their Brethren in New-York and New-England, that three of their old Friends, who had been carried Prisoners to France, were come with Proposals from Canada; that there was a Council of the Sachems appointed to meet at Onondaga, and that they therefore desired the Mayor of Albany, Peter Scheyler, and some others of their Brethren, to come thither, to be present and to advise on an Affair of so great Consequence; for they were resolved to do nothing without the Knowledge and Consent of all those that were included in the Chain with them.

The same Messenger told them, that some Letters were sent to the Jesuit at Oneydo; and that they would neither burn, nor suffer those Letters to be opened, till the Brethren should first see them.

All that the Magistrates of Albany did on this important Occasion, was to send three Indians with Instructions in their Name, to dissuade the Five Nations from entertaining any Thoughts of Peace, or yielding to a Cessation of Arms.

On the 4th of January one of the chief Mohawk Sachems came to Albany, to tell the Magistrates, that he was to go to Onondaga, and desired the Brethren's Advice how to behave there; on which the Magistrates thought it necessary to send likewise the publick Interpreter, and another Person to assist at the general Meeting, with written Instructions; but no Person of Note, that had any Influence on the Indians, went.

When the Messengers arrived at Oneydo, they discoursed privately with one of the Prisoners that had returned from France, and found that he had no Love for the French; but it is impossible but that Indians, who had seen the French Court, and many of their Troops, must be surprised at their Grandeur: he complained however of the ill Usage he had met with. The French chose, on this Occasion, to send first to Oneydo, because of the Assistance they expected the Jesuit, that resided there, would give to their Negotiation.

I believe it will not be tedious to the Reader, that desires to know the Indian Genius, if I give a circumstantial Account of this general Council or Parliament of the Five Nations, that he may see in what Manner a People that we call Savages behave on such important Occasions.

On the 22d of January the general Council was opened at Onondaga, consisting of eighty Sachems; in the first Place Sadekanaghtie, an Onondaga Sachem, rising up, addressed himself to the Messenger of Albany, saying,

Four Messengers are come from the Governor of Canada, *viz.* three who had been carried Prisoners to France, and a Sachem of the Praying Indians that live at Montreal.

The Governor of Canada notifies his Arrival to us, that he is the Count de Frontenac, who had been formerly Governor there; that he had brought back with him Tawerahet a Cayuga Sachem, and twelve Prisoners, that had been carried to France; then taking the Belt of Wampum in his Hand, and holding it by the Middle, he added, what I have said relates only to one Half of the Belt, the other Half is to let us know, that he intends to kindle again his Fire at Cadarackui next Spring, and therefore invites his Children, and Dekanasora an Onondaga Captain in particular, to treat there with him about the old Chain. Then Adarahta the chief Sachem of the praying Indians stood up, and said, with three Belts in his Hand, I advise you to meet the Governor of Canada as he desires; agree to this, if you would live, and gives one Belt of Wampum.

Tawerahet sends you this other Belt, to inform you of the Miseries, that he and the rest of your Countrymen have suffered in their Captivity; and to advise you to hearken to Yonondio, if you desire to live.

This third Belt is from Thurensera,* Ohguesse,† and Ertel,‡

---

* Thurensera signifies the Dawning of the Day, and was the Name given by the Indians to the Jesuit Lamberville, who had formerly resided at Onondaga.

† Monsr. le Morne, the Word signifies a Partridge.

‡ Ertel signifies a Rose, the Name of some other French Gentleman, for whom the Indians had an Esteem.

who say by it, to their Brethren: We have interceded for you with Yonondio, and therefore advise you to meet him at Cadarackui in the Spring, because it will be for your Advantage.

When this Sachem had done speaking, the Mohawk Messenger sent from Albany delivered his Message Word for Word, as he had received it, without omitting the least Article. The Interpreter, while the Indian was speaking, read over a Paper, on which the Message was set down, lest any Thing should have been forgot.

After this Cannehoot a Seneka Sachem stood up, and gave the general Council a particular Account of a Treaty made last Summer, between the Senekas and the Wagunha Messengers, (one of the Utawawa Nations) who had concluded a Peace for themselves, and seven other Nations, to which the other four Nations were desired to agree, and their Brethren of New-York to be included in it. He said the Proposals made in several Propositions were as follow.

1. We are come to join two Bodies into one. Delivering up at the same Time two Prisoners.

2. We are come to learn Wisdom of you Senekas, and of the other Five Nations, and of your Brethren of New-York. Giving a Belt.

3. We by this Belt wipe away the Tears from the Eyes of your Friends, whose Relations have been killed in the War, and likewise the Paint * from your Soldiers Faces. Giving another Belt.

4. We now throw aside the Ax, which Yonondio put into our Hands, by this third Belt.

5. Let the Sun, as long as he shall endure, always shine upon us in Friendship. Here he gave a red Marble Sun as large as a Plate.

6. Let the Rain of Heaven wash away all Hatred, that we

* The Indians always paint their Faces when they go to War, to make themselves look more terrible to the Enemy. A Soldier in the Indian Language is expressed by a Word, which signifies a Fair-fighter.

may again smoke together in Peace, giving a large Pipe of red Marble.

7. Yonondio is drunk, but we wash our Hands clean from all his Actions. Giving a fourth Belt.

8. Now we are clean washed by the Water of Heaven, neither of us must defile ourselves by hearkening to Yonondio.

9. We have twelve of your Nation Prisoners, who shall be brought home in the Spring; there he gave a Belt, to confirm the Promise.

10. We will bring your Prisoners when the Strawberries shall be in blossom,* at which Time we intend to visit Corlear, and see the Place where the Wampum is made. (New-York.)

The Speaker added, we will also tell our Friends the other Utawawa Nations, and the Dionondadies, who have eleven of your People Prisoners, what we have now done, and invite them to make Peace with you.

He said further, we have sent three Messengers back with the Wagunhas, in order to confirm this Peace with their Nation.

After the Seneka Speaker had done, the Wagunha Presents were hung up in the House, in the Sight of the whole Assembly, and afterwards distributed among the several Nations, and their Acceptance was a Ratification of the Treaty. A large Belt was given also to the Albany Messengers as their Share.

The Belt of Wampum sent from Albany was in like Manner hanged up, and afterwards divided.

New-England, which the Indians call Kinshon (that is a Fish) sent likewise the Model of a Fish, as a token of their adhering to the general Covenant. This Fish was handed round among the Sachems, and then laid aside to be put up.

After these Ceremonies were over, Sadekanahtie, an Onondaga Speaker, stood up, and said, Brethren, we must stick to our Brother Quider, and look on Yonondio as our Enemy, for

* The Indians in this Manner distinguish the Seasons of the Year, as the Time of planting Corn, or when it is ripe, when the Chesnuts blossom, &c.

he is a Cheat: By Quider they meant Peter Schyler the Mayor of Albany, who had gained a considerable Esteem among them; as they have no Labeals in their Language, they pronounce Peter by the Sound Quider.

The Messenger from Canada had brought Letters, and some medicinal Powder, for the Jesuit Milet, who resided at Oneydo. These Letters and the Powder were delivered to the Interpreter from Albany to be carried thither, that the Contents of them might be made known to the Sachems of the several Nations. The Jesuit was present all this While in their Council.

Then the Interpreter was desired to speak what he had to say from their Brethren at Albany. He told them, that a new Governor was arrived, who had brought a great many Soldiers from England. That the King of England had declared War against France, and that the People of New-England were fitting out Ships against Canada. He advised them, that they should not hearken to the French, for when they talk of Peace, said he, War is in their Heart, and desired them to enter into no Treaty but at Albany, for the French, he said, would mind no Agreement made any where else.

After this they had Consultations for some Time together, and then gave the following Answer by their Speaker.

Brethren, our Fire burns at Albany. We will not send Dekanasora to Cadarackui. We adhere to our old Chain with Corlear; we will prosecute the War with Yonondio, and will follow your Advice in drawing off our Men from Cadarackui. Brethren, we are glad to hear the News you tell us, but tell us no Lies.

Brother Kinshon, we hear you design to send Soldiers to the eastward against the Indians there; but we advise you, now so many are united against the French, to fall immediately on them. Strike at the Root, when the Trunk shall be cut down, the Branches fall of Course.

Corlear and Kinshon, Courage! Courage! In the Spring to

Quebeck, take that Place, and you'll have your Feet on the Necks of the French, and all their Friends in America.

After this they agreed to the following Answer to be sent to the Governor of Canada.

1. Yonondio, you have notified your Return to us, and that you have brought back 13 of our People that were carried to France, we are glad of it. You desire us to meet you at Cadarackui next Spring, to treat of the old Chain; but Yonondio, how can we trust you, after you have acted deceitfully so often? Witness what was done at Cadarackui; the Usage our Messengers met with at Utawawa, and what was done to the Senekas at Utawawa. This was their Answer; however, they sent a Belt with this, which always shews a Disposition to treat.

2. Therhansera, Oghuesse and Ertel, do you observe Friendship with us, if you have not, how come you to advise us to renew Friendship with Yonondio, they sent them likewise a Belt?

3. Tawerahet, the whole Council is glad to hear, that you are returned with the other twelve. Yonondio, you must send home Tawerahet and the others this very Winter, before Spring, and we will save all the French that we have Prisoners till that Time.

4. Yonondio, you desire to speak with us at Cadarackui: Don't you know that your Fire there is extinguished? It is extinguished with Blood, you must send home the Prisoners in the first Place.

5. We let you know that we have made Peace with the Wagunhas.

6. You are not to think, that we have laid down the Axe, because we return an Answer; we intend no such Thing: Our Far-fighters shall continue the War till our Countrymen return.

7. When our Brother Tawerahet is returned, then will we speak to you of Peace.

As soon as the Council broke up, their Resolutions were

made publick to all their People, by the Sachems of their several Nations.

Two Sachems were sent to Albany, by their general Council, to inform their Brethren there of their Resolutions, and to bring back the Contents of the Letters sent from Canada to the Jesuit.

As soon as they arrived, one of the Mohawks, that had been sent from Albany to the Council, delivered the Wagunha Belt, and repeated over distinctly all the Articles agreed to with that Nation, and referred to the Onondaga Speaker, being one of those sent by the Council of Albany, to recite the Answer to the Governor of Canada. He rising up, repeated over the whole as before set down, and added; The French are full of Deceit; but I call God to witness, we have hitherto used no Deceit with them, but how we shall act for the future, Time only can discover. Then he assured the Brethren, that the Five Nations were resolved to prosecute the War, in Token whereof he presented Quider * with a Belt, in which three Axes were represented. Perhaps by this Representation only three Nations joined in sending it, the Cayugas and Oneydoes being more under the Influence of the Jesuit Milet, who lived among them intirely, according to their Manner of Life, and was adopted by the Oneydoes, and made one of their Sachems. The Letters from Canada to him were read, they contained nothing but common News and Compliments.

The Mohawk Messengers, that had been sent from Albany, had carried with them Goods to sell at the general Council. This was taken Notice of at the general Council, and gave the Indians a mean Opinion of the People of Albany, and particularly of Peter Schyler; for it is exceedingly scandalous among the Indians, to employ a Merchant in publick Affairs; Merchants, (I mean the Traders with the Indians) are looked upon by them as Liars, and People not to be trusted, and of no Credit, who by their Thoughts being continually turned upon Profit and Loss, consider every Thing with that private

* Peter Schyler, Mayor of Albany.

View. As this made a Noise at Albany, by its giving the Jesuit an Opportunity of setting the Messengers from Albany in an ill Light, Peter Scheyler cleared himself by Oath, of his having any Interest directly or indirectly in those Goods, and sent a Belt back with his publick Justification. The Mohawk Messengers had refused to take the Goods, as being scandalous to the Business they went on; but were persuaded, by being told that the Goods belonged to Quider.

The Magistrates of Albany advised the Sachems, to send the Jesuit Prisoner to Albany, where he might be kept securely, without having it in his Power to do Mischief, but they could not prevail. The Indians were resolved to keep all the Means of making Peace in their own Hands.

CHAP. IV.

The French surprise Schenectady. The Mohawks Speech of Condoleance on that Occasion.

THE Count De Frontenac being desirous, as before observed, to raise the drooping Spirits of the French in Canada, by keeping them in Action, and engaging the most daring of them, in Enterprizes that might give Courage to the rest, had sent out three Parties against the English Colonies, in Hopes thereby to lessen the Confidence which the Five Nations had in the English Assistance, now that England had declared War against France. The Party sent against New-York was commanded by Monsr. De Herville, and was ordered to attempt the surprising of Schenectady, the nearest Village to the Mohawks; It consisted of 150 French Bush-lopers or Indian Traders, and of as many Indians, the most of them French Converts from the Mohawks, commonly called the Praying Indians, settled at a Place near Montreal, called Cahnuaga. They were well acquainted with all that Part of the Country round Schenectady; and came in Sight of the Place the 8th of February 1689–90.

The People of Schenectady were at that Time in the greatest Security, notwithstanding that they had Information from the Indians, of a Party of French, and French Indians being upon their March that Way. They did not think it practicable, in that Season of the Year, while it was extremely cold, and the whole Country covered with Snow. Indeed Europeans will hardly think it possible, that Men could make such a March through the Wilderness in the severest Frosts, without any Covering from the Heavens, or any Provision, except what they carried on their Backs.

Tho' the People of Schenectady were informed in the Evening before the Place was surprised, that several sculking Indians were seen near the Place, they concluded, that they could be only some of the neighbouring Indians; and as they had no Officer of any Esteem among them, not a single Man could be persuaded to watch in such severe Weather, tho', as the French owned afterwards, if they had found the least Guard or Watch, they would not have attempted the Place, but have surrendered themselves Prisoners: They were so exceedingly distressed with the Length of their March, and with Cold, and Hunger, but finding the Place in fatal Security, they marched into the Heart of the Village, without being discovered by any one Person; then they raised their War Shout, entered the Houses, murdered every Person they met, Men, Women, and Children, naked and in cold Blood; and at the same Time set Fire to the Houses. A very few escaped, by running out naked into the Woods in this terrible Weather: And several hid themselves, till the first Fury of the Attack was over; but these were soon driven from their lurking Places by the Fire, and were all made Prisoners.

Captain Alexander Glen, at this Time, lived at a Distance by himself, on the other Side of the River, and was the most noted Man in the Place. He had at several Times been kind to the French, who had been taken Prisoners by the Mohawks, and had saved several of them from the Fire. The French were sensible what Horror this cruel sacking of a defenceless Place, and murdering People in cold Blood, must raise in Mens Minds; and to lessen this, they resolved to shew their Gratitude to Captain Glen. They had passed his House in the Night, and observing that he stood on his Defence the next Morning, some of them went to the River Side, and calling to him, assured him, that they designed him no Injury. They persuaded him to come to the French Officer, who restored to him all his Relations that were Prisoners.

Some Mohawks being also found in the Village, the French dismissed them, with Assurance, that they designed them no Hurt.

This Conduct was not only necessary to promote the Peace which the Count De Frontenac with so much Earnestness desired, but likewise to secure their Retreat, by making the Mohawks less eager to pursue them.

The French marched back, without reaping any visible Advantage from this barbarous Enterprize, besides the murdering sixty-three innocent Persons in cold Blood, and carrying twenty-seven of them away Prisoners.

The Care the French took to sooth the Mohawks had not intirely it's Effect, for as soon as they heard of this Action, a hundred of their readiest young Men pursued the French, fell upon their Rear, and killed and took twenty-five of them.

This Action frightened the Inhabitants in and about Albany so much, that many resolved to desert the Place, and retire to New-York. They were packing up and preparing for this Purpose, when the Mohawk Sachems came to Albany to condole, according to their Custom, with their Friends, when any Misfortune befals them. I shall give their Speech on this Occasion, as it will be of Use to the Reader, in order to his forming a true Notion of the Indian Genius. They spoke the twenty-fifth of March as follows.

"Brethren, the Murder of our Brethren at Schenectady by the French grieves us as much, as if it had been done to our selves, for we are in the same Chain; and no Doubt our Brethren of New-England will be likewise sadly affected with this cruel Action of the French. The French on this Occasion have not acted like brave Men, but like Thieves and Robbers. Be not therefore discouraged. We give this Belt *to wipe away your Tears.*

"Brethren, we lament the Death of so many of our Brethren, whose Blood has been shed at Schenectady. We don't think that what the French have done can be called a Victory, it is only a farther Proof of their cruel Deceit. The Governor of Canada sends to Onondaga, and talks to us of Peace with our whole House, but War was in his Heart, as you now see by woful Experience. He did the same formerly at Cadarackui, and in the Senekas Country. This is the third Time he has acted so deceitfully. He has broken open our House at both Ends, formerly in the Senekas Country, and now here. We hope however to be revenged of them. One Hundred of our bravest young Men are in Pursuit of them, they are brisk Fellows, and they will follow the French to their Doors. We will beset them so closely, that not a Man in Canada shall dare to step out of Doors to cut a Stick of Wood; But now *we gather up our Dead, to bury them,* by this second Belt.

"Brethren, we came from our Castles with Tears in our Eyes, to bemoan the Bloodshed at Schenectady by the Perfidious French. While we bury our Dead murdered at Schenectady, we know not what may have befallen our own People, that are in Pursuit of the Enemy, they may be dead; what has befallen you may happen to us; and therefore *we come to bury our Brethren at Schenectady* with this third Belt.

"Great and sudden is the Mischief, as if it had fallen from Heaven upon us. Our Forefathers taught us to go with all Speed to bemoan and lament with our Brethren, when any Disaster or Misfortune happens to any in our Chain. Take this Bill of Vigilance, that you may be more watchful for the future. *We give our Brethren Eye-Water* to make them sharp sighted, giving a fourth Belt.

"We are now come to the House where we usually renew the Chain; but alas! we find the House polluted, polluted with Blood. All the Five Nations have heard of this, and we are come to wipe away the Blood, and clean the House. We come to invite Corlear, and every one of you, and Quider (calling to every one of the principal Men present by their Names) *to be revenged of the Enemy,* by this fifth Belt.

"Brethren, be not discouraged, we are strong enough. This is the Beginning of your War, and the whole House have their Eyes fixed upon you at this Time, to observe your Behaviour. They wait your Motion, and are ready to join in any resolute Measures.

"Our Chain is a strong Chain, it is a Silver Chain, it can neither rust nor be broken. We, as to our Parts, are resolute to continue the War.

"We will never desist, so long as a Man of us remains. Take Heart, do not pack up and go away,* this will give Heart to a dastardly Enemy. We are of the Race of the Bear, and a Bear you know never yields, while one Drop of Blood is left. *We must all be Bears;* giving a sixth Belt.

"Brethren be patient, this Disaster is an Affliction which has fallen from Heaven upon us. The Sun, which hath been cloudy, and sent this Disaster, will shine again with its pleasant Beams. Take Courage, said he, Courage, repeating the Word several Times as they gave a seventh Belt."

(*To the English.*)

Brethren, three Years ago we were engaged in a bloody War with the French, and you encouraged us to proceed in it. Our Success answered our Expectation; but we were not well begun, when Corlear stopt us from going on. Had you permitted us to go on, the French would not now have been able to do the Mischief, they have done, we would have prevented their sowing, planting or reaping.

* This was spoke to the English, who were about removing from Albany.

We would have humbled them effectually, but now we dye. The Obstructions you then made now ruin us. Let us after this be steady, and take no such false Measures for the future, but *prosecute the War vigorously.* Giving a Bever Skin.

The Brethren must keep good Watch, and if the Enemy come again, send more speedily to us. Don't desert Schenectady. The Enemy will glory in seeing it desolate. It will give them Courage that had none before, *fortify the Place,* it is not well fortified now: The Stockadoes are too short, the Indians can jump over them. Gave a Bever Skin.

Brethren, The Mischief done at Schenectady cannot be helped now; but for the future, when the Enemy appears any where, let nothing hinder your sending to us by Expresses, and fire great Guns, that all may be alarmed. We advise you to bring all the River Indians under your Subjection to live near Albany, to be ready on all Occasions.

Send to New-England, tell them what has happened to you. They will undoubtedly awake and lend us their helping Hand. It is their Interest, as much as ours, to push the War to a speedy Conclusion. Be not discouraged, the French are not so numerous as some People talk. If we but heartily unite to push on the War, and mind *our Business, the French will soon be subdued.*

The Magistrates having returned an Answer on the twenty seventh, to the Satisfaction of the Indians, they repeated it all over, Word by Word, to let the Magistrates see how carefully they minded it, and then added,

Brethren, we are glad to find you are not discouraged. The best and wisest Men sometimes make Mistakes. Let us now pursue the War vigorously. We have a hundred Men out, they are good Scouts. We expect to meet all the Sachems of the other Nations, as they come to condole with you. You need not fear our being ready, at the first Notice. Our Ax is always in our Hands, but take Care that you be timely ready. Your Ships, that must do the principal Work, are long a fitting out. We do not design to go out with a small Company, or in sculking Parties; but as soon as the Nations can meet, we shall be ready with our whole Force. If you would bring this War to a happy Issue, you must begin soon, before the French can recover the Losses they have received from us, and get new Vigour and Life, therefore send in all Haste to New-England. Neither you nor we can continue long in the Condition we are now in, we must order Matters so, that the French be kept in continual Fear and Alarm at home; for this is the only Way to be secure, and in Peace here.

The Scahkok Indians, in our Opinion, are well placed where they are (to the Northward of Albany); they are a good Out-guard; they are our Children, and we shall take Care that they do their Duty: But you must take Care of the Indians below the Town, place them nearer the Town, so as they may *be of most Service to you.*

Here we see the Mohawks acting like hearty Friends, and if the Value of the Belts given at that Time be considered, together with what they said on that Occasion, they gave the strongest Proofs of their Sincerity. Each of these Belts amount to a large Sum in the Indian Account.

The English of New-York and the French of Canada were now entering into a War, in which the Part the Five Nations are to take is of the greatest Consequence to both; the very Being of the French Colony depended on it, as well as the Safety of the English. The Indians at this Time had the greatest Aversion to the French, and they desired nothing so much, as that the English might join heartily in this War. We shall see by the Sequel how a publick Spirit, directed by wise Counsels, can overcome all Difficulties, while a selfish Spirit loses all, even natural Advantages. In the present Case, the Turn Things took seems to have been entirely owing to one Thing. The French in making the Count de Frontenac Governor of Canada, chose the Man every Way the best qualified for this Service: The English seemed to have little Regard to the Qualification of the Person they sent, but to gratify a Relation or a Friend, by giving him an Opportunity to make a Fortune; and as he knew that he was recommended with this View, his Counsels were chiefly employed for this Purpose.

By this Means an English Governor generally wants the Esteem of the People; while they think that a Governor has not the Good of the People in View, but his own, they on all Occasions are jealous of him; so that even a good Governor, with more Difficulty, pursues generous Purposes and publick Benefits, because the People suspect them to be mere Pretences to cover a private Design. It is for this Reason, that any Man, opposing a Governor, is sure to meet with the Favour of the People, almost in every Case. On the other Hand, the Opinion the French had of the Count de Frontenac's publick Spirit, and of his Wisdom and Diligence, made them enter into all his Measures without hesitating, and chearfully obey all his Commands.

CHAP. V.

The Five Nations continue the War with the French; the Mohawks incline to Peace; their Conferences with the Governor of New-York.

THE Governor of Canada received Hopes that the Five Nations inclined to Peace, by their returning an Answer to Therawaet's Message, and thought he might now venture to send some French to them with further Proposals. The Chevalier D'O, with an Interpreter called Collin, and some others, went; but they had a much warmer Reception than they expected, being forced to run the Gauntlet through a long Lane of Indians, as they entered their Castle, and were afterwards delivered up Prisoners to the English.

The Five Nations kept out at this Time small Parties, that continually harassed the French. The Count de Frontenac sent Captain Louvigni to Missilimakinak, to relieve the Garison, and he had Orders, by all Means, to prevent the Peace which the Utawawas and Quatoghies were upon the Point of concluding with the Five Nations. He carried with him one hundred forty three French, and six Indians, and was likewise accompanied with a Lieutenant and thirty Men, till he got one hundred twenty Miles from Montreal. They were met in Cadarackui River, at a Place called the Cats, by a Party of the Five Nations, who fell vigorously on their Canoes, killed several of the French, and made them give Way; but Louvigni, by putting his Men ashore, at last got the better, after a smart Engagement, in which the Indians had several Men killed, and two Men, and as many Women, taken Prisoners. I am obliged to rely on the French Account of these Skirmishes; they do not mention the Number of the Indians in this Rencounter, but I suspect them to have been much fewer than the French; for when the Enemy are equal in Number, or greater, they seldom forget to tell it. One of the Indian Prisoners was carried by them to Missilimackinak, to confirm this Victory, and was delivered to the Utawawas, who eat him. The Lieutenant carried the other back with him. He was given to Therawaet.

To revenge this Loss, the Five Nations sent a Party against the Island of Montreal, who fell on that Part called the Trembling Point; and though they were discovered before they gave their Blow, they attacked a Party of regular Troops, and killed the commanding Officer, and twelve of his Men: Another Party carried off fifteen or sixteen Prisoners from Riviere Puante, over against Trois Rivieres. This Party was pursued, and finding that they were like to be overpowered, murdered their Prisoners and made their Escape. These Incursions kept all the River, from Montreal to Quebeck, in continual Alarm, and obliged the Governor to send all the Soldiers to guard the south Side of the River. Notwithstanding this, five Persons were carried away in Sight of Sorel Fort,

by a small skulking Party, but they were soon afterwards recovered by the Soldiers. About the same Time another Party
burnt the Plantations at St. Ours.

The Five Nations had conceived great Hopes from the Assistance of the English, as the Magistrates of Albany had
promised the Mohawks, when they came to condole, after the
surprising of Schenectady; but the English were so far from
performing these Promises, that many of the Inhabitants
retired from Albany to New-York; and they who had the Administration of Affairs, were so intent on their party Quarrels,
that they intirely neglected the Indian Affairs. Indeed the People of New-York have too often made large Promises, and have
thereby put the Indians upon bold Enterprizes, when no
Measures were concerted for supporting them. This made
the Indians think, that the English were lavish of Indian
Lives and too careful of their own. The Mohawks, who lived
nearest the English, were most sensible of these Things, and
soon entertained Notions prejudicial to the Opinion they
ought to have had of the English Prudence and Conduct;
it is even probable, these Indians began to entertain a mean
Opinion of both the English Courage and Integrity. It is not
strange then, that the Mohawks at last gave Ear to the as-
siduous Application of their Countrymen, the praying Indians,
who, with French Arguments, persuaded them to make Peace
as soon as possible, without trusting longer to the English,
who had so often disappointed or deceived them.

The Mohawks sent one of their Sachems, Odigacege, to the
praying Indians, who introduced him to the Count de Frontenac. The Count made him welcome, and told him, that he
was sorry for the Injuries his Predecessors had done them; but
that he would treat them like Friends, if their future Conduct
did not prevent him, and gave him a Belt, with Proposals of
Peace to his Nation.

Colonel Slaughter, who was then Governor of New-York,
being informed that the Five Nations were like to make Peace
with the French, by their having lost much of their Confidence

in the English Assistance, found it necessary to meet them, which he did in the End of May 1691. There were present at that Time six Oneydo, eleven Onondaga, four Cayuga, and ten Seneka Sachems. He renewed the Covenant with them, and gave them Presents. The Mohawks having entered into a Treaty with the French, did not join with the other four Nations in their Answer.

On the second of June the Speaker, in Name of the other four Nations, told him, they were glad to see a Governor again in this Place; that they had learned from their Ancestors, that the first Ship which arrived in this Country surprized them exceedingly; that they were curious to know what was in its huge Belly. They found Christians in it, and among them one Jacques, with whom they made a Chain of Friendship, which has been preserved to this Day. By that Chain it was agreed, that whatever Injury was done to the one, should be deemed, by both Sides, as likewise done to the other. Then they mentioned the Confusion that had lately been in the Government of New-York, which had like to have confounded all their Affairs, but hoped all would be reduced to their wonted Order and Quiet. They complained of several of the Brethren leaving Albany in Time of Danger, and praised those by Name who staid, and then said: Our Tree of Peace, which grows in this Place, has of late been much shaken, we must now secure and fasten its Roots; we must frequently manure and dress it, that its Roots may spread far.

They assured the Governor, that they were resolved to prosecute the War against the French as long as they lived, and that they would never speak of Peace, but with the common Consent. They abhor those that do otherwise, and desired that the Brethren might not keep a Correspondence with Canada by Letters. You need not (said they) press us to mind the War, we mind it above all Things; do you but your Parts, lay aside all other Thoughts but that of the War, for it is the only Thing we have at Heart. They gave Bevers at the End of every distinct Part of their Answer.

On the fourth the Mohawks spoke to the Governor, in Presence of the other four Nations: They confessed the Negotiations they had with the Praying Indians, and with the Governor of Canada, and that they had received a Belt from him. Then they restored one of the Prisoners taken at Schenectady, as the Fruit of that Negotiation. They desired the Governor's Advice, and the Advice of the whole House, what Answer to return to the Governor of Canada; and lastly, desired the Senekas to release the Prisoners they had taken from the Praying Indians.

Colonel Slaughter check'd the Mohawks for entering into a separate Treaty with the Enemy, and said he could admit of no Proposals of Peace. He told them, that the Prisoners taken from the Praying Indians must not be restored; putting them in mind, that some of them having been formerly released, soon after returned and murdered several People, and burnt several Houses.

He assured them of his Assistance, and then added, You must keep the Enemy in perpetual Alarm. The Mohawks thanked him for his Assurance of Assistance; but took Notice of his saying, *You* must keep the Enemy in perpetual Alarm. Why don't you say, they replied, We will keep the Enemy in perpetual Alarm. In the last Place, the Mohawks renewed their League with all the English Colonies; adding, Though an angry Dog has endeavoured to bite the Chain in Pieces, we are resolved to keep it firm, both in Peace and in War: We now renew the old Chain, that so the Tree of Peace and Prosperity may flourish, and spread its Roots through all the Country.

In the last Place, the four Nations answered the Mohawks.

"Mohawks, our Brethren, in answer to your Proposals from the Governor of Canada, we must put you in Mind of his Deceit and Treachery; we need only give one recent Instance, how he lately sent to the Senekas to treat of Peace, and at the same Time fell upon Schenectady, and cut that Place off. We tell you, that the Belt sent by the French Governor is Poison;

we spew it out of our Mouths, we absolutely reject it, and are resolved to prosecute the War as long as we live." Then they left the Belt lying on the Ground.

CHAP. VI.

The English attack Montreal by Land, in Conjunction with the Indians, and Quebeck by Sea.

IT was now evident that the Indians could no longer be amused with Words, and that, unless the English entered soon upon Action, the French would carry their Design of making Peace with the Five Nations, and the English be left to carry on the War in America by themselves. Certainly a more proper Opportunity of doing it with Success could not be expected, than at present, while the French in Canada had neither recovered their Spirits, nor the Strength they had lost, by the terrible Incursions of the Five Nations. A joint Invasion on Canada was concerted with New-England, they were to attack Quebeck by Sea, while New-York attacked Montreal by Land. The Governor therefore proposed to the Indians to join with him in attacking Canada, for which Purpose he told them, that he designed to send a considerable Force this Summer. They desired Time to consult on it at their general Meeting, which was soon to be held at Onondaga, and to know what Number of Christians he designed to send, that they might join a suitable Number of their Men. To this the Governor answered, that he must not communicate the Particulars of his Design to so many, because they could not then be kept secret from the Enemy; as he found by the Discoveries that were last Year made to the French by that Means.

It was at last agreed, that the Mohawks should join with the Christians that were to march from New-York directly against Montreal, and that the other four Nations should send a considerable Party down Cadarackui Lake, and join them before Montreal.

Major Peter Schuyler, the same whom the Indians call Quider, commanded the Party sent from New-York, which consisted of three hundred Men, one half Christians, the other Mohawks and Scahkook Indians. He set out from Albany about Midsummer. As he was preparing his Canoes to pass Corlear's Lake, he was discovered by the French Indians, who immediately returned to Montreal, to give Information of what they had seen. The Chevalier Clermont was sent out to make further Discoveries: He found the English above Chamblie, and went immediately back with the Intelligence he there gained. In the mean while Mr. de Callieres, Governor of Montreal, did all in his Power to give Major Schuyler a proper Reception, by drawing the Militia and regular Troops together for the Defence of the Place. There happened to be a very considerable Number of Utawawas trading at that Time at Montreal, Mr. de Colliere, in Order to engage them to join him, made a great Feast for them, went among them, and, after the Indian Manner, began the war Song, leading up the Dance with his Axe in his Hand, and shouting and hollowing in the same wild Manner the Indians do. This done, he carried his whole Force, which consisted of twelve hundred Men, cross the River, and encamped on the south Side, at la Prairie de la Magdeleine, together with a great Number of Utawawas, the Praying Indians, and other French Indians. The famous Therawaet being now entirely gained by the Caresses of the Count de Frontenac, made one of the Number. They encamped round the Fort, which stood on a steep rising Ground between two Meadows.

Major Schuyler having left forty of his Men to guard his Canoes, which had carried him cross the Lake, marched on without stopping. He got into a Hollow, which led into the Meadow, without being discovered; and marching under that Cover, he fell suddenly upon the Militia, who were soon put into Confusion, and many of them, and of the Utawawas, who were posted with them, were killed. He pursued them as they fled to the Fort, which he attacked briskly, but was obliged to leave it, by the Approach of the regular Troops who came to relieve it. He received them however bravely, and, after they had lost several Officers and many Men, they retired. Major Schuyler finding the Number of the Enemy much greater than was expected, and being informed that a considerable Party of the Enemy had marched Southward, he began to apprehend, that this Party was sent to cut off his Retreat, by destroying his Canoes. It was resolved therefore immediately to follow this Party; he overtook them, and they covering themselves behind some large fallen Trees, he attacked them, and made his Way through them, but with considerable Loss.

In this Attack the Mohawks signalized themselves, but the Scahkook Indians did not behave themselves well. The Mohawks, upon no Occasion, yielded an Inch of Ground, till the English first gave Way. The French, by their own Accounts, lost, in the several Attacks made by Schuyler, two Captains, six Lieutenants, and five Ensigns, and, in all, three hundred Men, so that their Slain were in Number more than Major Schuyler had with him. The Mohawks suffered much, having seventeen Men killed, and eleven wounded. They returned to Albany the eleventh of August.

After the English under Major Schuyler had retired, an Owenagunga Indian came from New-England, with an Account of the Preparations made there against Canada, and that they had actually sailed.

This Fleet, which was commanded by Sir William Phips, was discovered in St. Laurence Bay, while the Count de Frontenac remained at Montreal; and thereupon he made all possible Haste to Quebeck, and carried three hundred Men with him.

The Fleet, which consisted of thirty Sail, did not reach Quebeck till the seventh of October. Sir William spent three

Days in nothing but Consultation, while the French made all possible Preparation for a Defence, and, by this Means, suffered them to get over the Fright and Consternation, into which the first Appearance of the Fleet had thrown them; for the Place was not in any Posture of Defence. It gave them Time likewise to draw all the Country round them into the Town. And on the fourth Day Sir William summoned the Count to surrender, who returned him such an Answer as his Conduct deserved.

The English landed four Miles below the Town, and had thick Woods to march through, before they could come at it, in which Ambuscades of French and Indians were made at proper Distances, by whom the English were repulsed with considerable Loss. They attempted the Wood again the next Day with no better Success.

The French, in their Account of this Action, say, that the Men, though they appeared to be as little disciplined as Men could be, behaved with great Bravery, but that Sir William's Conduct was such, that, if he had been in Concert with them, he could not have done more to ruin the Enterprize; yet his Fidelity was never suspected. In short, this Descent was so ill managed, that the English got on Board again in the Night, with the Loss of all the Cannon and Baggage which they had landed.

The French thought themselves in such great Danger at that Time, that they attributed their Deliverance to the most immediate Protection of Heaven, in confounding the Devices of their Enemy, and by depriving them of common Sense; and for this Reason the People of Quebeck make an annual Procession, in Commemoration of this Deliverance.

Sir William cannonaded the Town for some Time with little Execution, and then returned in Haste, Winter approaching; indeed that Season was already so far advanced, that he lost eight Vessels in his Return.

The Five Nations continued their Incursions all along St. Laurence River, from Montreal to Quebeck, and carried away many Scalps. At one Time a French Officer, with thirty eight Men, surprised some of the Five Nations in a Cabin, which they had built near Lake St. Piere. Some of them escaped and informed two other Cabins, which the French had not discovered, and they returned with their Companions, and killed the Captain and Lieutenant, and one half of the Men.

Notwithstanding that the French preserved their Country, these warlike Expeditions, and the Necessity they were under of being on their Guard, prevented their cultivating the Ground, or of reaping the Fruit of what they had sowed or planted. This occasioned a Famine in Canada, and, to increase the Misery of the poor Inhabitants, they were forced to feed the Soldiers gratis, while their own Children wanted Bread.

In October the Onondagas, Cayugas, and Oneydoes came to Albany, to condole with the English, for the Men lost in the Expedition against Montreal, as they had already done with the Mohawks. They said it was ever their Custom to condole with their Friends when they lost any Number of Men in Battle, though they had the Victory. They at the same Time, as they had often done before, complained of the Dearness of Powder: Why, say they, do you call us your King's Soldiers, when you will not sell us Powder at the usual and reasonable Rates?

And in answer to a Complaint, of there not being a sufficient Number of English sent against Montreal, the People of Albany upbraided them with a Breach of Promise, in not sending that Party down Cadarackui River which they promised, which they said was the chief Reason of the want of Success in that Expedition.

CHAP. VII.

The French and the Five Nations continue the War all Winter with various Success. The French burn a Captain of the Five Nations alive.

THE old French Governor kept up his Vigour and Spirits wonderfully, no Fatigue made him ever think of Rest. He knew of what Use it would be to convince the Five Nations, that the joint Attack of the English and Indians had neither weakened him, nor frightened him from carrying on the War with as much Vigour as before. It was absolutely necessary that the Utawawas and other Western Indians, who came to Montreal to trade, should return safe to their own Country, otherwise there would be an End to the French Trade with those Nations, upon which the Being of Canada depends; for it is only by the Fur-trade with these Nations that they make Returns to Europe; and if these Nations did not return in Time, all the Western Indians would look on the French as lost, and consequently would make Peace with the Five Nations, and perhaps join in the Destruction of Canada.

Captain la Forest, with one hundred and ten Men, was sent to conduct the Utawawas Home; he carried with him considerable Presents sent by the King of France, to confirm these Nations in the French Interest.

Two Indian Prisoners, taken at la Prairie, were given to the Utawawas, and carried with them, to confirm the Stories they were to tell of their Successes against the English and Five Nations. These poor Men were there burnt alive; and if I should add, that it was done by French Instigation, what I shall relate by and by will clear me of the want of Charity. I believe it was so, in Order to rivet the Hatred between these People and the Five Nations.

The Five Nations continued their Incursions all Winter on Canada. Forty of the Mohawks fell upon Fort Vercheres, and carried off twenty of the Inhabitants; but the Alarm reaching Montreal, Mr. de Crizaei, with one hundred Men of the regular Troops, was sent in pursuit of them, who recovered most of the Prisoners.

The Count de Frontenac being informed, that a considerable Party of the Five Nations hunted Bever on the Neck of Land between Cadarackui Lake and Lake Erie, with great Security, resolved to give them a better Opinion of the Strength and Courage of the French. For this Purpose he sent three hundred and twelve Men to surprise them, under the Command of Mr. Beaucour, a young Gentleman. The Praying Indians of Montreal were of the Party. This Expedition being in the Winter, they were obliged to undergo cruel Fatigues, while they marched on the Snow with snow Shoes, and carried all their Provision on their Backs. Several of the French had their Feet frozen, which obliged fifteen to return, with some old Indians, that could not bear the Fatigue; and it was with much Difficulty that Beaucour could persuade the rest to continue their March. After a March to a surprizing Distance, at that Season of the Year, they surprised eighty of the Five Nations, who notwithstanding made a brave Defence, and did not run before they left most of their Men dead on the Spot. Three Women were made Prisoners, with whom the French immediately turned back to Montreal. Some stragling Parties went towards Albany, but did no more Mischief than killing two or three stragling Persons, and alarming the Country.

The Trade to Missilimakinak being still intirely stopt, by the Parties of the Five Nations investing Cadarackui River, by which, and Cadarackui Lake, the Passage in Canoes is made to the Western Indians, Captain la Noue, with a Command of the regular Troops, was ordered early in the Spring to guard the Traders through that Passage; but when he reached the Falls de Calumette, he discovered the Enemy, and returned faster than he went.

La Noue had Orders a second Time to attempt this Passage,

and went as far as the River du Lievre (thirty Leagues from Montreal) without any Obstruction; but there discovering several Canoes of the Five Nations, he went back as fast as before.

The Quatoghies and the Bullheads * having informed the French of another smaller River, which falls into Cadarackui River, and runs to the Northward of it, by which a Passage might be made to the Lakes, it was resolved to attempt this Passage, though it were much farther round, and more dangerous, there being many more rapid Falls in that River. Three Officers, with thirty Soldiers, were sent with the Traders for this Purpose, but a Party of the Five Nations meeting with them in the long Fall, before they reached this River, they were all killed or taken, except four that escaped back to Montreal.

A considerable Party of the Five Nations, under the Command of Blackkettle, a famous Hero, continued a long Time on Cadarackui River, in hopes of meeting with other French Parties, in their Passage towards Missilimakinak; but finding that no Attempts were made that Way, he resolved to make an Irruption into the Country round Montreal. The French say he had six hundred Men with him; but they usually increase the Number of their Enemies, in the Relation they give of these Transactions, either to excuse their Fears, or to increase their Glory.

Blackkettle overrun the Country (to use the French Expression) as a Torrent does the Low-lands, when it overflows its Banks, and there is no withstanding it. The Soldiers had Orders to stand upon the defensive within their Forts. Mr. de Vaudreuil pursued this Party (after they had burnt and ravaged the whole Country) at the Head of four hundred Men; he overtook them and surprised them. The Five Nations fought desperately, though the same Author, at this Place, makes them no more than two hundred Men. After they had lost twenty Men on the Spot, they broke through the French,

* The Bullheads are said to be cowardly People.

and marched off. The French lost four Officers and many common Soldiers, and they took five Men, nine Women, and five Children Prisoners.

The Five Nations in a few Days had however some Revenge; a Captain having had Orders to guard the Vessels from Montreal to Quebeck, a Party of the Five Nations attacked him in his Return, as he passed through the Islands in Lake St. Pierre. He himself was killed, and the whole Party intirely routed.

The French all this Summer were obliged to keep upon the defensive within their Forts, while the Five Nations, in small Parties, ravaged the whole Country, so that no Man stirred the least Distance from a Fort, but he was in danger of losing his Scalp.

The Count de Frontenac was pierced to the Heart, when he found that he could not revenge these terrible Incursions of the Five Nations; and his Anguish made him guilty of such a Piece of monstrous Cruelty, in burning a Prisoner alive after the Indian Manner, as though I have frequently mentioned to have been done by the Indians, yet I forbore giving the Particulars of such barbarous Acts, suspecting it might be too offensive to Christian Ears, even in the History of Savages. Here however I think it useful to give a circumstantial Account of this horrid Act, to shew on one Hand, what Courage and Resolution, Virtue, the Love of Glory, and the Love of one's Country can instill into Mens Minds, even where the Knowledge of true Religion is wanting; and on the other Hand, how far a false Policy, under a corrupt Religion, can debase even great Minds.

The Count de Frontenac, I say, condemned two Prisoners of the Five Nations to be burnt publickly alive. The Intendant's Lady intreated him to moderate the Sentence, and the Jesuits, it is said, used their Endeavours for the same Purpose. But the Count de Frontenac said, there is a Necessity of making such an Example, to frighten the Five Nations from approaching the Plantations, since the Indulgence, that had hitherto been shewn, had incouraged them to advance with the greatest Boldness to the very Gates of their Towns; while they thought they run no other Risque, but of being made Prisoners, where they live better than at Home. He added, that the Five Nations having burnt so many French, justified this Method of making Reprizals. But with Submission to the Politeness of the French Nation, may I not ask, whether every (or any) horrid Action of a barbarous Enemy, can justify a civilized Nation in doing the like?

When the Governor could not be moved, the Jesuits went to the Prison, to instruct the Prisoners in the Mysteries of our Holy Religion, *viz.* of the Trinity, the Incarnation of our Saviour, the Joys of Paradise, and the Punishments of Hell, to fit their Souls for Heaven by Baptism, while their Bodies were condemned to Torments. But the Indians, after they had heard their Sentence, refused to hear the Jesuits speak, and began to prepare for Death in their own Country Manner, by singing their Death Song.

Some charitable Person threw a Knife into the Prison, with which one of them dispatched himself: The other was carried out to the Place of Execution by the Christian Indians of Loretto, to which he walked, seemingly, with as much Indifference as ever Martyr did to the Stake. While they were torturing him, he continued singing, that he was a Warrior brave and without Fear; that the most cruel Death could not shake his Courage; that the most cruel Torment should not draw an indecent Expression from him; that his Comrade was a Coward, a Scandal to the Five Nations, who had killed himself for fear of Pain; that he had the Comfort to reflect, that he had made many Frenchmen suffer as he did now. He fully verified his Words, for the most violent Torment could not force the least Complaint from him, though his Executioners tried their utmost Skill to do it. They first broiled his Feet between two red hot Stones; then they put his Fingers into red hot Pipes, and though he had his Arms at Liberty, he would not pull his Fingers out; they cut his Joints, and taking hold of the Sinews, twisted them round small Bars of Iron. All this while he kept singing and recounting his own brave Actions against the French. At last they flead his Scalp from his Skull, and poured scalding hot Sand upon it; at which Time the Intendant's Lady obtained Leave of the Governor to have the *Coup-de-grace* given, and I believe she thereby likewise obtained a Favour to every Reader, in delivering him from a further continuance of this Account of French Cruelty.

Notwithstanding this Cruelty, which the French Governor manifested towards the Five Nations, and thereby his Hatred of them, he found Peace with them so necessary to Canada, that he still pursued it by all the Means in his Power. For this Purpose the Praying Indians (who, as I observed before, are Mohawks, and have always kept a Correspondence with their own Nation) were employed to bring it about, and to endeavour a Cessation of Arms, that the Governor might have an Opportunity of shewing what kind Things he had in his Heart towards the Five Nations, but without Success.

CHAP. VIII.

The Five Nations treat with Captain Ingoldsby.

THE Governor of New-York, Colonel Slaughter's Death, soon after his Arrival, was very prejudicial to the Affairs of New-York; for Captain Ingoldsby, who had no other Commission but that of Captain of one of the Independent Companies of Foot, took upon himself the Government of the Province, without any Authority; and he having likewise highly offended a great Number of the People, by the Share he took in the late Party Quarrels, it was not easy for him to prosecute any vigorous Measures. He was reckoned to be much more a Soldier than a Statesman.

Captain Ingoldsby met the Five Nations at Albany, the sixth of June 1692. In his Speech, he told them of his vigorous Resolutions to prosecute the War, and then blamed them for not sending (according to their Promise) a Party down Cadarackui River, to join them that went from Albany against Montreal, and for their Carelessness in suffering themselves to be surprised last Winter in their Hunting. He desired them to keep the Enemy in perpetual Alarm, by the Incursions of their Parties into the Enemy's Country, and to give him timely Notice of all their Motions. He told them in the next Place, that he heard the French were still using their wonted Artifice, of amusing them with Offers of Peace; but the former Proceedings of the French sufficiently demonstrates, said he to the Brethren, that while Peace is in their Mouths, War is in their Hearts, and the late horrid Murder of the Brethren, after Quarter given, sufficiently shews the Perfidy and Rancour of their Hearts. It is in vain, said he, to think of any Cessation of Arms, much less of a Peace, while the two Kings are at War at Home. He added, Virginia is ready to assist us, and only waits the King's Orders, which are daily expected, and then renewed the Chain for Virginia. In the last Place he told them, that he heard the Dionondadas had sent two Prisoners Home, with a View thereby to procure Peace; and advised them by all Means to make Peace with that Nation.

The Five Nations answered by Cheda, an Oneydo Sachem:

"Brother Corlear,

The Sachems of the Five Nations have with great Attention heard Corlear speak; we shall make a short Recital, to shew you with what Care we have hearkened. After the Recital he continued.

We heartily thank Corlear, for his coming to this Place to view the Strength thereof, for his bringing Forces with him, and for his Resolution of putting Garisons into the Frontier Places. Giving five Bevers and a Belt.

Brother Corlear, as to what you blame us for, let us not

reproach one another, such Words do not savour well among Friends. They gave nothing with this Article.

Brother Corlear, be patient under the Loss of your Men, as we are of the Mohawks our Brethren, that were killed at the same Time. You take no Notice of the great Losses we have suffered. We designed to have come to this Place to have condoled with you in your Loss, but the War took up all our Time, and employed all Hands. They gave five Bevers, four Otters, and one Belt, as a Gift of Condolence.

Brother Corlear, we are all Subjects of one great King and Queen, we have one Head, one Heart, one Interest, and are all ingaged in the same War. You tell us, that we must expect no Peace while the Kings are at War on the other Side the great Water. We thank you for being so plain with us. We assure you we have no Thoughts of Peace. We are resolved to carry on the War, though we know we only are in danger of being Losers. Pray do you prosecute the War with the same Resolution. You are strong and have many People. You have a great King, who is able to hold out long. We are but a small People, and decline daily, by the Men we lose in this War, we do our utmost to destroy the Enemy; but how strange does it seem to us! How unaccountable! that while our great King is so inveterate against the French, and you are so earnest with us to carry on the War, that Powder is now sold dearer to us than ever? We are poor, and not able to buy while we neglect hunting; and we cannot hunt and carry on the War at the same Time: We expect, that this Evil we so justly complain of be immediately remedied. Giving nine Bevers.

Brother Corlear, you desire us to keep the Enemy in perpetual Alarm, that they may have no Rest, till they are in their Graves; Is it not to secure your own Frontiers? Why then not one Word of your People that are to join us? We assure you we shall continue to carry on the War into the Heart of the Enemies Country. Giving eight Bevers.

We the Five Nations, Mohawks, Oneydoes, Onondagas, Cayugas, and Senekas, renew the Silver Chain whereby we are linked fast with our Brethren of Assarigoa (Virginia) and we promise to preserve it as long as the Sun shall shine in the Heavens. Giving ten Bevers.

But Brother Corlear, How comes it, that none of our Brethren fastened in the same Chain with us, offer their helping Hand in this general War, in which our great King is engaged against the French? Pray Corlear, how come Maryland, Delaware River, and New-England, to be disengaged from this War? You have always told us, that they are our Brethren, Subjects of the same great King. Has our King sold them? Or do they fail in their Obedience? Or do they draw their Arms out of our Chain? Or has the great King commanded, that the few Subjects he has in this Place, should make War against the French alone? Pray make plain to us this Mystery? How can they and we be Brethren, and make different Families? How can they and we be Subjects of the same great King, and not be engaged in the same War? How can they and we have the same Heart, the same Head, and the same Interest, as you tell us, and not have the same Thoughts? How comes it, that the Enemy burns and destroys the Towns in New-England, and they make no Resistance? How comes our great King to make War, and not to destroy his Enemies? When, if he would only command his Subjects on this Side the great Lake to joyn, the Destruction of the Enemy would not make one Summer's Work.

You need not warn us of the Deceit and Treachery of the French, who would probably insinuate Thoughts of Peace; but Brethren, you need not fear us, we will never hearken to them: Tho' at the same Time, we must own, that we have not been without Thoughts of your being inclined to Peace, by Reason of the Brethrens Backwardness in pushing on the War. The French spread Reports among us to this Purpose, and say, that they had in a Manner concluded the Matter with you. We rejoice to be now assured of this Falshood. We shall never desist fighting the French as long as we shall live. And gave a Belt of Wampum.

We now renew the old Chain, and here plant the Tree of Prosperity and Peace. May it grow and thrive, and spread its Roots even beyond Canada. Giving a Belt.

We make the House clean, where all our Affairs of Importance are transacted with these five Otters.

We return you Thanks for the Powder and Lead given us; but what shall we do with them without Guns, shall we throw them at the Enemy? We doubt they will not hurt them so. Before this we always had Guns given us. It is no Wonder the Governor of Canada gains upon us, for he supplies his Indians with Guns as well as Powder; he supplies them plentifully with every Thing that can hurt us. Giving five Otters.

As to the Dionondadas setting two of our Nation at Liberty, we must tell you, that it was not the Act of that Nation, but the private Act of one Person: We are desirous to make Peace with that Nation as soon as we can, upon honourable Terms. And gave a Belt.

The Mohawks, before they left the Place, desired a private Conference with the Governor, and told him, that they were all exceedingly dissatisfied, that the other English Colonies gave no Assistance, and that it might prove of ill Consequence. Captain Ingoldsby promised to write to them, and hoped it would have a good Effect.

CHAP. IX.

The French surprise and take three Mohawk Castles.

THE Praying Indians promised their Endeavours to reconcile their Brethren the Mohawks to the French, on whom the French expected they would have much Influence; but their

Endeavours proving ineffectual, their Correspondence began to be suspected. The French thought they did more Hurt than Good, by the Intelligence the Enemy by their Means received. The French in Canada began to lose their Spirits, by being obliged to remain so long upon the defensive, as the Five Nations gained more Courage by it. The Count de Frontenac thought it therefore absolutely necessary to undertake some bold Enterprize, to shew the Five Nations, that they had to do with an Enemy still able to act offensively: An Attack on the Mohawks he thought would be most effectual for this Purpose, because it would shew, at the same Time, that the English would not protect their nearest Neighbours. As this was designed to be done by Surprize, the Winter Season was chosen for this Purpose, as least to be suspected at such a Time; and when the Enemy could not, without great Hardship, keep Scouts abroad, to discover them or the English give any Assistance.

The Body of the French designed for this Expedition was put under three Captains of the regular Troops, and thirty Subalterns, and consisted of picked Men of the regular Troops of the common Militia of the Country of the Praying Indians, the Quatoghies of Loretto, Adirondacks, and Sohokies, who live to the eastward of Boston, making in all about six or seven hundred Men, so that a great Part of the Force of Canada was employed in it. They were well supplied with all Sorts of Ammunition, Provision, Snow-shoes, and such Conveniencies for Carriage, as were practicable upon the Snow, and through such great Forests as they had to pass. The French at Canada have a Kind of light Sledges made with Skins, and are drawn by large Dogs on the frozen Snow.

They set out from la Prairie de Magdaleine the 15th of January 1692–3, after having endured what might have been thought unsurmountable Hardships; they passed by Schenectady at some Distance from it, on the 8th of February, at which Time one that had been taken Prisoner, when that

Place was sacked, made his Escape from them, and gave the People of Schenectady Intelligence of the French, who by an Express, immediately informed the Commandant of Albany. The Millitia was expeditiously raised, and a Lieutenant with fifty five Horse was immediately dispatched to Schenectady; but no Care was taken to give the Mohawks Notice, which might have been done without much Danger, by sending up the South Side of the River, whilst the French marched on the North. The French, on the 8th at Night, reached the first Mohawk Castle, where there were only five Men, and some Women and Children in great Security, their other Men being all abroad, these were all taken without Opposition. The next Fort not far from it was in like Manner surprized, without any Opposition, both of them were very small, and being next the English, not fortified.

Schenectady being the nearest English Settlement to the Mohawks, and but a little Way from their nearest Castle, many of them are always there. The Mohawks then in the Town were exceedingly enraged, that none went out to assist their Nation; some were sent therefore out the next Day, to gain Information of the Enemy, and to give the Mohawks Notice; but they returned without doing their Duty.

The French went on to the next Mohawk Fort, which was the largest; and coming to that in the Night, they heard some Noise, and suspected they were discovered: But this Noise was only occasioned by a War Dance, forty of the Indians designing to go next Day upon some Enterprize. The French approached the Castle silently, and finding the Indians no way on their Guard, opened the Gate, and entered before they were discovered; but notwithstanding this, and the Confusion the Indians must be in, this Conquest was not without Loss of Blood, the French having lost thirty Men, before the Indians entirely submitted: The French designed to have put them all to the Sword, but their own Indians would not suffer it, and gave Quarter: They took three hundred Prisoners, of whom one hundred were fighting Men. I have no Account of the Number of Mohawks killed, but no Doubt it was very considerable.

When the Account came to Albany, how much the Mohawks, who were at Schenectady, were enraged, that no Assistance was sent to their Countrymen; Peter Schuyler a Major of the Militia offered himself to go with what Force could be got ready for their Assistance. He went himself immediately to Schenectady, and sent out to discover the Enemy: His Scouts brought him Intelligence, first, that the French were in Possession of the two smallest Forts, afterwards, that they had heard great Firing at the largest Fort; and at last, that it was taken. Having received 200 Men, partly regular Troops, but most of the Militia, he began his March on the 12th in Quest of the Enemy; but hearing soon after, that six hundred Men of the upper Castles were on their March, 'tis probable he did not endeavour to be up with the French so soon as he might; for I find by his Journal, that he was nearer them on the fourteenth, than he was two Days after. He had not sufficient Force to fight them: He sent therefore to the upper Indians, to hasten their March. On the 15th he was joined by these Indians, in all two hundred and ninety Men and Boys, very ill armed. His Body then consisted of two hundred and fifty Christians, and two hundred and ninety Indians, armed fighting Men. They had no other Provision but some Biscuit every Man had in his Pocket. On the 16th he was informed by an Indian, who pretended to be a Deserter, that the French had built a Fort, where they designed to wait for him, and fight him; whereupon he sent an Express to Coll. Ingoldesby, then Commandant at Albany, to hasten more Men to join him, with sufficient Provision for the whole. He found afterwards, that this Indian was sent by the French, on purpose to persuade the Indians to give over the Pursuit. Major Schuyler came up to the Enemy on the 17th; when he came near them he did not go on streight towards them, for Fear of Ambuscades, but marched round. As soon as he came in Sight, he was saluted with three loud Shouts, which were answered with as much Noise. The Indians began in their Manner to secure themselves, by felling the Trees between them, and the Enemy sallied out to prevent them, but were soon beat back. The Indians fell to Work again, and desired the Christians to assist them, which was done, but in such Confusion, that they themselves were in Danger from the falling Trees. The French sallied a second Time with all their Force, crying out, *They run, we'll cut them off, and get their Provisions;* but they were warmly received, and beat back into their Fort. They sallied a third Time, and were beat back with considerable Loss, the Indians bringing in several Heads and Scalps. As soon as the Skirmishing was over, the Major sent back an Express, to hasten the Men that were to reinforce him, and were to bring Provision, some of the Men having had no Provision for two Days. The Major then secured himself, under the Cover of the fallen Trees, and kept out Watches to observe the French.

The 18th proving a cold stormy Day, with Snow, he was informed, by a Deserter, that the French were upon their March, it not being easy to follow their Tracks, or to discover them in such Weather. The Officers were commanded to pursue and retard their March, till the Reinforcement should come up, but the Men refused to march without Provision. The Officers, with about 60 Men, and a Body of Indians, followed the Enemy till Night, when they began to secure themselves, by fortifying their Camp. The Officers wanting a sufficient Number to secure themselves in like Manner, or to fight the Enemy, returned, leaving about forty Christians, and one hundred Indians, to observe them. On the 19th the Provisions, with about 80 Men, arrived, under the Command of Captain Sims of the regular Troops. Every Man, as he was served with Provision, marched towards the Enemy. The Van was commanded by Captain Peter Matthews of the regular Troops, who coming up with the Enemy's Rear, would have attacked them, to retard their March, but the Mohawks were averse to fighting. The French dropt on purpose several of their Prisoners, who told the Mohawks, that the French were resolved to put all the Prisoners to the Sword, if they should be attacked. The Enemy passed the North Branch of Hudson's River upon a Cake of Ice, which, very opportunely for them, stuck there in one Place, while it was open by a late Thaw, both above and below. The Weather continuing very cold, and the Indians averse to fighting, Major Schuyler gave over the Pursuit on the 20th, having lost only four private Men, and as many Indians, two Officers and twelve Men Christians and Indians were wounded. The French lost thirty three Men (the Bodies of twenty seven were found) of whom four were Officers, and twenty-six wounded, as the Deserters told him. Between forty and fifty Prisoners were recovered. I have been told, that Captain Matthews desired Coll. Schuyler, when he came first up with the French, to summon them to surrender; he said, the French are in great Distress, and this will give them an Opinion of our Strength; but Coll. Schuyler refused, tho' he was brave, he was no Soldier; and it is very probable, that the French observing the want of Conduct and Discipline, were encouraged. It is true, the English were in great Want of Provisions at that Time. The Indians eat the Bodies of the French that they found. Coll. Schuyler (as he told me himself) going among the Indians at that Time, was invited to eat Broth with them, which some of them had ready boiled, which he did, till they, putting the Ladle into the Kettle to take out more, brought out a French Man's Hand, which put an End to his Appetite.

The French went home as fast as they could carry their wounded Men with them; but coming to a Place, where they had hid Provisions for their Supply in their return, they found it all spoiled. This put them in great Distress, so that they were forced to eat their Shoes; they sent some of the nimblest Men forward to Montreal, that Provision might meet them. As soon as they came near the Settlements they dispersed, every Man running home to eat, so that they returned to Canada like an Army routed. The French own they lost eighty Men, and had thirty three wounded in this Expedition.

One may wonder how it is possible for Men to march several hundred Miles in the Wilderness, while the Ground is every where covered with Snow, two or three Feet deep at least; but the foremost march on Snow Shoes, which beat a firm Track for those that follow. At Night, when they rest, they dig a Hole in the Snow, throwing the Snow up all round, but highest towards that Side from whence the Wind blows, so large, as to contain as many Men as can lye round a Fire: They make the Fire in the Middle, and cover the frozen Ground round it with the small Branches of the Fir-Trees. Thus they tell me a Man lyes much warmer, than one imagines that never tried it.

When the Information of the French came to Schenectady, an Express was sent to New-York to Coll. Fletcher then Governor there; the Express reached New-York, an hundred and fifty Miles from Albany, the 12th at ten in the Night. The Governor got the City Regiment under Arms by eight the next Morning.

He called out to know who were willing to go with him to the Frontiers, they all immediately threw up their Hats, and answered one and all. Indeed the People of this Province have, upon all Occasions, shewn their Courage and Resolution in Defence of their Country; but the Misfortune is, they are under no Discipline, and have been seldom led by Men that knew their Duty. The Governor ordered an hundred and fifty Voluntiers for this Service, and as many more from Long-Island. The River then happened to be open by a sudden Thaw, which does not, at that Time of the Year, happen once in twenty Years. He embarked three hundred Men in five Sloops, by four in the Afternoon of the 14th, and arrived at Albany the 17th at nine in the Morning. The same Day the Governor went to Schenectady, and ordered the Men to follow, but before they could get every Thing ready for their March into the Woods, they had an Account, that Major

Schuyler was upon his Return. Several Gentlemen of Albany, particularly Mr. Lanslear, a Gentleman of the best Estate there, went out Voluntiers under Major Schuyler, which I ought not to have forgot.

Coll. Fletcher made a Speech to the Mohawks at Albany, he blamed their supine Negligence, in suffering themselves to be surprised in the Manner they were in Time of War. He told them that they had Reason to be convinced, that the English were their Friends heartily, by the Number of Men he had marched to their Assistance in a very little Time, upon the first Notice. He promised to wipe away their Tears in the Spring, by considerable Presents; and that he would, in the mean while, take Care of their Subsistence, by providing Houses and Victuals for them. He told them, he doubted they had some false Brethren among them, that gave the French Information, and favoured their Designs; and in the last Place, advised them to convince the French, that they had not lost their Courage with this Misfortune.

The Mohawks, in their Answer, called Coll. Fletcher by the Name of Cayenguirago; and he was called so by the Indians always after this. It signifies a great swift Arrow, as an Acknowledgement of the Speed he made to their Assistance. But they appeared, in their Answer, to be quite disheartened; they had not, in the Memory of any Man, received such a Blow. They said their Strength was quite broke, by the Continuance of the War; but they added, if all the English Colonies would join, they could still easily take Canada: Their being so ill armed, was the Reason (they said) that the French had now escaped.

The French, continued they, arm their Indians compleatly, and furnish them with every Thing necessary for War, as we find every Time we meet with them.

The French had got a great Quantity of Furs, and other Peltry, at Missilimakinak, by their Trade with the Indians; but the Five Nations had so effectually blocked up the Passage between that and Canada, that they had remained there useless to the French for several Years. The Count de Frontenac, after his Success against the Mohawks, was in Hopes the Five Nations would keep more at home in Defence of their own Castles, and with these Hopes sent a Lieutenant, with eighteen Canadians, and twenty praying Indians, to open the Passage to Missilimakinak; but this Party fell in with another of the Five Nations, who entirely routed them, so that a few escaped only, to give an Account of their Misfortune; at last 200 Canoes, loaded with Furs from Missilimakinak, arrived at Montreal, which gave as universal a Joy to Canada, as the Arrival of the Galleons give in Spain.

CHAP. X.

The Treaties and Negotiations the Five Nations had with the English and French, in the Years 1693 and 1694.

AS by this Time the Reader may be tired with the horrid Scenes of a barbarous War, it may be some Relief to observe the Indian Genius in the Arts of negotiating; and see how a barbarous People, without any of the Arts and Sciences in which we value our selves, manage their Interest with the most learned, most polite, and artificial Nation in Europe. The Five Nations were informed, that the Governor of Canada had received from Europe a very considerable Recruit of Soldiers, and of all Sorts of Ammunition. This, with the great Loss the Mohawks had lately suffered, while they had been amused by the English with great Hopes, and very little real Assistance, made the Oneydoes, at last yield to the Solicitations of the Jesuit Milet, to send a Message to the French for Peace. It is probable he had the Art to influence the People at Albany to favour his Designs, by giving them Hopes of being included in the Peace, as may be conjectured, from what will appear in the Sequel.

Coll. Fletcher being informed, that the Oneydoes had sent a Messenger to Canada, sent for the Five Nations to Albany. He spoke to them the third of July 1693.

He first excused his not meeting them as he had promised, at the Time the Sap begins to run in the Trees, by Reason of his having received a Commission to be Governor of Pensilvania, to which Place he was obliged at that Time to go. He put them in Mind with what Speed he came to their Assistance last Winter, and how effectual, in all Probability, it would have been, had they only retarded the Enemy's March till he could have reached them: He advised them to guard against being drunk, and shewed them the ill Consequences of it in Time of War.

Then he said, "I have received Information, that some of the Brethren are wavering, and inclined to Peace with the Enemy; and am assured, that such Thoughts must arise from the Instigation of the Jesuit Milet, whom some of the Brethren have suffered to live so long among them, and whose only Practice is to delude and betray them. Let me therefore advise you to remove that ill Person from among you."

In the End he condoled their Dead, and made them a very considerable Present of ninety Guns, eight hundred and ten Pound of Powder, eight hundred Bars of Lead, a Thousand Flints, eighty seven Hatchets, four Gross of Knives, besides a considerable Quantity of Cloathing and Provisions. This Present, he told them, their King and Queen had sent them, and renewed the Covenant for all the English Colonies.

The King usually sends them a considerable Present with every new Governor sent to New-York, which is not always applied as it is designed. If this Present had been made sooner, it had been of much more Use to the English, as well as to the Five Nations.

The Five Nations the next Day spoke as follows.

"Brother Cayenguirago,

"We are involved in a bloody War, which makes us sit in Sorrow and Grief; and being about to speak of Matters of Importance, we, in the first Place, clear the Mouth and Throat of our Interpretess, by giving her these three Bever Skins."

Then they repeated his Excellency's Speech, in Answer to which they said,

"Brother Cayenguirago, we rejoice, that the great King and Queen of England take such Notice of us, as we find, by the large Present sent us; we return hearty Thanks for the Ammunition especially.

"We are glad that our Brother Cayenguirago renews the Chain, not only between us and this Government, but likewise with New-England, Virginia, Maryland and Pensilvania; it shall be kept inviolable by us the Five Nations, as long as the Sun shines. We pray our Brother Cayenguirago to have a watchful Eye, that none of the other Colonies keep any Correspondence with the Enemy, but use their Endeavours to destroy them. We heard nothing of what you told us of the Priest Milet, who lives at Oneydo, till we came to this Town. We have enquired the Truth of our Brethren the Oneydoes, who confess, that the Priest sent an Indian to Canada with Letters, which has surprised us very much.

"Brother Cayenguirago, you are our great Tree, whose Roots extend to the utmost Bounds of this Government; we desire you may not be disturbed when any of our Prisoners misbehave, for they are not countenanced by us; and all proper Methods shall be taken, to prevent the like for the future. In like Manner we beg you to take Care, that none of the Prisoners you have correspond with the Enemy, as we suspect the Chevalier D' O. did; and that he was sent with Letters to Canada by some of our Brethren. (He made his Escape from Boston.)

"Brother Cayenguirago, In former Times our Propositions to one another were only Discourses of Peace and Friendship, and in giving Presents; but how much is the Case altered of late? Now we talk of nothing but War, and are continually prompting one another to it. As to our Parts, we will keep close to the War to the last Drop of our Blood; and tho' we be tossed to and fro with Storms, we will remain stedfast to the last Man, as it was resolved by both in the Beginning of the War.

"Brother Cayenguirago, we were told in our own Country, not only that the King had made you Governor of Pensilvania, but likewise that you were preparing a Fleet to take Canada. O! what joyful News this was to our young Men. Sadagarus, the great Seneka Captain, was to command them. Now they said, we need only make one hearty Push, while the Fleet is before Quebeck. Now there will be an End to this bloody War, and all our Troubles; But alas, now we are come here, we hear not one Word of this Design.

"Brother Cayenguirago, you are that flourishing Tree that covers us; you keep the Chain bright; we have one Request to make to you, that you may stay with us, and not return to England; for you know our Ways and Manners. If you have any Thing to tell the King and Queen, write it to them, for the King knows you to be a wise Man, and will therefore believe you.

"Brother Cayenguirago, we are very glad to hear that Pensilvania is come under your Government, bring their young Men here, with their Bows and Arrows and Hatchets in their Hands, for this is the Place of Action. We are pleased that the Showonons or Satanas, who are our Enemies, have applied to you for Protection; and that you sent them to us to endeavour a Peace, and that you sent Christians with them, to conduct them back again. We wish they were come to assist us against the common Enemy.

"Brother Cayenguirago, now we have done, but must tell you again, that we roll and wallow in Joy, by Reason of the great Favour the great King and Queen has done us, in sending us Arms and Ammunition, at a Time when we are in the greatest Need of them; and because there is such Unity among the Brethren."

They made the Governor a considerable Present of Furs, to shew their Respect to his Person; but they did not give one Belt to confirm any one Article; so that the whole of it is, according to their Stile, only argumentative.

Coll. Fletcher not being satisfied with their Answer, concerning the Jesuit Milet, made this further Proposal to them. "As to Milet the Priest, whom the Brethren of Oneydo still harbour among them, I must tell you again, that he betrays you, and all your Councils; and that you may see I desire not to diminish your Number, I am willing to give you a pretty Indian Boy, in Lieu of the old Priest; and accordingly the Boy was brought and delivered to them.

In answer to this the Oneydo Sachem said, "As soon as the Indian Messenger returns all his Papers shall be taken from him, and be forthwith brought to our Brother Cayenguirago, before the Priest shall see any of them: we are willing to take the Boy in Exchange for the Priest, but it is not safe to do it, while our Messenger is in the Power of the Enemy; let the Boy stay here till we bring the Priest, which shall be as soon as the Messenger shall return." But he gave no Belt, or other Present, to confirm this Promise. He added,

"Brother Cayenguirago, we now acquaint you that it is proposed by all the Five Nations, to make Peace with the Dionondadies, a Nation of Indians near in Alliance with the French of Canada. This will both strengthen us and weaken the Enemy. The Senekas, who live nearest them, have undertaken this Treaty, and take Belts of Wampum from the other Nations, to confirm the Peace. We desire your Approbation, that you would send your Belt in Concurrence, as our eldest Brother in our Chain."

The Governor approved of this, and gave them a Belt to carry in his Name.

Notwithstanding what the Speaker of the Five Nations had

promised to the Governor, to bring all the Papers the Oneydo Messenger should bring from Canada, before the Jesuit Milet should have Liberty to see them, it could not be difficult for the Jesuit, to persuade them to keep the Power of making Peace in their own Hands, and for that Purpose, to call a Meeting of the Sachems of Onondago, where all such Matters had been formerly transacted among themselves, and there to determine independently, rather than to submit themselves to another Nation at Albany. They only invited the English to assist at the general Council. The English used what Arguments they could to dissuade this Meeting, but rather to observe the Promise made to the Governor; and it seems used some Threatning. The Mohawks had so much Regard to the English, that they refused to assist at the Council. The other four, notwithstanding this, met, and resolved on an Answer to be sent to the Governor of Canada; but at the same Time, to shew their Regard to the Mohawks and English, these Resolutions were not to be final, till they should first be communicated to the English and Mohawks, and their Advice received thereon; for which Purpose several Sachems were sent to Albany, of whom Decanesora was the Principal and the Speaker.

Decanesora had for many Years the greatest Reputation among the Five Nations for speaking, and was generally employed as their Speaker, in their Negotiations with both French and English: He was grown old when I saw him, and heard him speak; he had a great Fluency in speaking, and a graceful Elocution, that would have pleased in any Part of the World. His Person was tall and well made, and his Features, to my thinking, resembled much the Bustos of Cicero. I shall give an Account of these Negotiations from Decanesora's Mouth, because his Narration agrees in the main with the Account the French give of them, and carries along with it as strong Evidences of Truth, as that of the French do: but the chief Reason is, that I intend to give the Reader as perfect a Notion as I can of the Indian Genius; and here it will appear, what Art Decanesora had, to make an Account of an Affair less disagreeable to English Ears, which had been undertaken against their Advice, and contrary to their Interest.

Decanesora spoke to Major Schuyler (Quider) and the Magistrates of Albany, the second of February 1693-4 as follows.

"Brother Cayenguirago,* we are come to acquaint you, that our Children the Oneydoes having of themselves sent a Messenger to Canada, he has brought back with him a Belt of Peace from the Governor of Canada.

"As soon as Tariha (the Messenger) arrived at Canada, he was asked, where the six hundred Men were that were to attack Canada, as they had been informed by Cariokese a Mohawk Deserter? He assured them there was no such Design.

"He was carried to Quebeck, where he delivered his Belt, with the following Propositions. Onondio, if you would have Peace go to Albany, and ask it there, for the Five Nations will do nothing without Cayenguirago. The Governor of Canada was angry at this, and said, he had nothing to do with the Governor of New-York, he would treat only with the Five Nations; the Peace between the Christians must be made on the other Side the great Lake. He added, he was sorry to see the Five Nations so far degenerated, as to take a sixth Nation into their Chain, to rule over them. If you had desired me to come and treat in any of your Castles, I would have done it; but to tell me I must go to Albany, is to desire of me what I can by no Means do. You have done very ill, to suffer the People of New-York to govern you so far, that you dare do nothing without their Consent. I advise you to send two of each Nation to me, and let Decanesora be one of them. I have Orders from the King my Master to grant you Peace, if you come in your proper Persons to ask it. The Governor of Canada afterwards said,

"Children of the Five Nations, I have Compassion for your

* When the Affair of which they speak concerns the Government of New-York, the Indians always address themselves to the Governor, whether he be present or not.

little Children, therefore come speedily, and speak of Peace to me, otherwise I'll stop my Ears for the future: By all Means let Decanesora come; for if the Mohawks come alone, I will not hear them, some of all the Five Nations must come. Now Tariha return home, and tell the Five Nations, that I will wait for their coming till the Trees bud, and the Bark can be parted from the Trees. I design for France in the Spring, and I leave a Gentleman to command here, to whom I have given Orders to raise Soldiers, if you do not come in that Time, and then what will become of you? I am truly grieved to see the Five Nations so debauched and deceived by Cayenguirago, who is lately come to New-York, and by Quider. Formerly the chief Men of the Five Nations used to converse with me; but this Governor of New-York has so deluded you, that you hearken to none but him; but take Care of what will follow, if you hearken to none but him."

Then Decanesora excused the not sending the Letters to Albany, which came by Tariha, as they had promised, saying, the other Nations trusted this to the Oneydoes, because the Messenger was to return to them, and the Oneydoes deceived the others. He likewise excused their not coming to Albany as soon as Tariha returned, which was in November. He said the chief Sachem of the Onondagas, who was entrusted (as their Speaker) by the Five Nations with their general Affairs, by the general Council of Onondaga, had a sore Leg, and could not travel.*

That in such Case he (Decanesora) did all that was in his Power, that is, he called a Council at Onondaga, to give Directions in this Affair; and that he invited Quider to this Council. He continued,

"The four Nations that met there resolved to send Deputies to Canada, and that I Decanesora was to be one of them; but at the same Time ordered me, with some others, to communicate the Resolutions of the General Council to our

* This, in the Indian Idiom, signifies a trifling excuse of an unwilling person.

Brethren at Albany, and to the Mohawks, to be farther advised by them.

"The Resolutions are, to send three Belts to the Governor of Canada, with the following Propositions.

"I. Onondio, you have sent for me often, and as often asked, why I am afraid to come? The great Kettle of War that you have hung over the Fire is the Reason of it. Then laying down the first Belt, I am to ask his Consent to the other two Belts which I still keep in my Hand.

"II. We now not only throw down the Kettle, and thereby throw the boiling Water out of it, but likewise break it to Pieces, that it may never be hanged up again by this second Belt.

"III. Hearken, Onondio, you are sent from the French King, your Master, as Cayenguirago is from the great King and Queen of England. What I am now about to speak to you, is by Inspiration from the great God of Heaven. You say that you will have nothing to do with our Brethren of Cayenguirago, but I must tell you, that we are inseparable, we can have no Peace with you so long as you are at War with them; we must stand and fall with them; which I am to confirm, by laying down the third Belt.

"When this was concluded the Jesuit Milet, and another French Gentleman (who had been taken Prisoner, and was taken into the Place of the chief Sachem of Onondaga, formerly lost in the War, and thereby became a Sachem) desired Leave to add two Belts to the other three. By their being Sachems they had a Vote in the General Council, and a Right to propose any Thing. They wrote and read to us the Purports of their Belts, and we have brought their Papers with us, to shew to our Brethren."

To shew the Necessity they were under of making Peace, speedily he added:

"That two Women, who were Prisoners at Canada, had made their Escape, on Purpose to inform them that the French were making great Preparations of Battoes, and other Necessaries for an Expedition; one said, she had informed one of the Sachems of the Praying Indians of her Design, who sent an Indian with her to advise the Five Nations, to prevent the great Danger they were threatened with by a speedy Conclusion of the Peace; and added, that they had sent one of their People back with this Praying Indian, to assure them that Deputies would certainly go to Canada in the Spring to treat of Peace." I make no Doubt, this was only an Article to hasten the Five Nations to conclude the Peace, lest the English, if it were delayed, should find Means to prevent it. Then he shewed the Flag which the Governor of Canada sent them to be carried by their Deputies, that the French might know them. Upon these Resolutions being taken, the Five Nations recalled six hundred Men, that they had placed along Cadarackui River, to intercept the French, as they passed to and from Missilimakinak.

The Jesuit's Papers being read to them, several Things were found in them which he had not read to the General Council. To this Decanesora answered; "We know that the Priest favours his own Nation, and deceives us in many Things; but it is not in his Power to alter our Affection to our Brethren, we wish you would bury all Misunderstandings that you have conceived on his Account; and we likewise wish you gave less Credit to the Rum-Carriers than you do." Here we see, by this Appellation, what a contemptible Character the Traders have among the Indians, and yet the Government of New-York has almost perpetually trusted the Management of the Indian Affairs to these Traders.

Decanesora ended his Conference as follows: "The Governor of Canada's Words, and the Resolutions of the four Nations are now before you, consult therefore what is to be done, and if it be necessary for the Brethren to go to our Castles to advise us farther, be not unwilling; and then he laid down a large Belt eleven Rows deep, and seven Fathom of Wampum."

The next Day Major Schuyler told them that he could consent to no Treaty with the French; but proposed to them to meet the Governor here in seventy Days, and that Decanesora in particular should return at that Time, and gave a Belt.

They agreed to meet the Governor at that Time; "But as for myself (says Decanesora) I cannot promise; I am now the Minister of the General Council, and cannot dispose of myself, but by their Directions; if they order me, I shall willingly return. We did not expect to hear such positive Prohibition of keeping any Correspondence with the French; seventy Days must pass before we meet again, if any Mischief be done by the Enemy in that Time, let us not blame one another. Consider again what is most for the publick Good, and let it be spoken before we part, and laid down a large Belt of fourteen deep."

Major Schuyler then asked them again, whether they promised to stop all Correspondence with the French, either by the Jesuit or otherwise, for seventy Days, and till they shall have his Excellency the Governor's Answer.

Decanesora answered to this, "I have no Authority to answer this Question. I shall lay the Belt down in every one of the Castles, and tell, that by it all Correspondence is desired to stop with the French; but I cannot promise that this will be complied with."

Major Schuyler on the sixth called the Indians again together: He advised them not to submit to, nor trust such a perfidious Nation as the French are, who have upon all Occasions proved themselves such. Be not discouraged, (says he, giving a Belt) Heaven begins again to favour us. This Day the Forerunners of the Shawonons are come to Town, seven Nations are on their March following them, one Thousand in Number, including Men, Women and Children, as you may learn from their own Mouths. Take Courage, and be not afraid, giving five Fathom of Wampum. This seemed a lucky Incident, and accordingly it had more Influence than all other Arguments together.

Decanesora, the next Day, called the Magistrates together, and told them, you have at last shut up the Way to Canada, but we have one Thing to ask, after mature Deliberation, which we expect will not be refused us. Major Schuyler assured them that every Thing should be granted, which was either for their Safety or Honour. We desire then, said he, that you send a Messenger along with ours to the Praying Indians at Canada, to tell them that the Priest is false; that we are to meet Cayenguirago in the Spring, and therefore cannot go to Canada at that Time; and that a further Cessation of Arms be agreed to, till such Time as we can go. We desire at least, that if you will not send a Messenger, that you put the Message in Writing, as a Token of your Assent to it. This last was agreed to, and the Message was put in Writing in the following Words, and translated into French.

The Dispatch of three Belts, which two Messengers of the Five Nations carry to the Caraguists and Catholick Indians, according to what was resolved by the Agayandres or Sachems of the Five Nations, at Albany, February the ninth 1694.

First Belt.

The Agayandres of the Five Nations cannot go to Canada in the Spring, as they gave Reason to expect by the last Message from Onondaga, because Cayenguirago has called all the Five Nations, and other Indians, to meet him at Albany, in the Month of April next, to which the Five Nations have agreed.

Second Belt.

If the Caraguists, or French, have any Thing to propose to the Five Nations, they may safely come into our Country. This Belt opens the Path, and secures it to them both coming and going.

Third Belt.

The Five Nations, and their Friends, lay down the Hatchet till they shall have an Answer, which they expect in forty Days. Provided nevertheless, that the Caraguists and French tye their Hatchets down at the same Time.

These Belts were accordingly presented to the Praying Indians of Cahnuaga, who refused to receive them but in the Presence of Mr. de Callieres, Governor of Montreal. Mr. de Callieres acquainted the Count de Frontenac with the Contents. After which the Praying Indians, in Presence of Mr. de Callieres, gave the following Answer.

"We will have no Correspondence with the Five Nations, but by Order of the Governor of Canada our Father, and unless Decanesora, and the other Deputies, come before the Feast of St. John, the Way will be shut up for ever after, and our Father's Ears will be stopt. We however assure you, that if the Deputies come in that Time the Path shall be safe both coming and going."

Whether the Accounts given of the coming of the Shawonons was only an Amusement, or whether they were diverted on their March, I know not, for I find no farther Account of them in the Register of the Indian Affairs: However it was, the Impression, made on the Indians by that News, was not sufficient to withstand the Force of the resolute Answer their Messenger received from the Praying Indians. Decanesora and the other Deputies went early in the Spring to Canada; the other Sachems met Colonel Fletcher at Albany, the fourth of May 1694. The Indians spoke first by Sadakanahtie, an Onondaga Sachem, as follows:

"Brother Cayenguirago,
"Some of our Sachems agreed last Winter that we should keep no Correspondence with the French; we confess that

we have broke that Promise, and that we have received a Messenger from Canada, and have sent our Deputies likewise thither. The Belt is not yet arrived, by which we are to acknowledge our Fault in doing this. The Reason of our doing it is truly this, we are afraid of the Enemy.

"When a Messenger came last Year from Canada to Onondaga, our Brother Cayenguirago discharged our Meeting in General Council at Onondaga, to consult on that Message, and ordered us to hold our General Council here at Albany on that Affair. The Privilege of meeting in General Council, when we please, is a Privilege we always have enjoyed; no former Governor, of the Name of Corlear, ever obstructed this Privilege. We planted a Tree of Peace in this Place with them, its Roots and Branches extend as far as Virginia and New-England, and we have reposed with Pleasure under its Shade. Brother, let us keep to that first Tree, and let us be united and unanimous; such Prohibition of our Assemblies will be of ill Consequence, and occasion Differences between us.

"We acknowledge, I say, our sending Agents to Canada for Peace, we were incouraged in doing this, by the Knowledge we have of the Governor of Canada. He is an old Man, and was formerly Governor of that Place. He was always esteemed a wise peaceable Man, and therefore we trust our Message will have a good Issue. We did not take it amiss that you sent to the Dewagunhas, nor that Arnout was sent to the Satanas, both of them our Enemies; and, for the same Reason, our Brother Cayenguirago ought not to be displeased with our sending to the French for Peace.

"We, Onondagas, acknowledge ourselves to have been the chief Promoters of this Message, we have sent in all nine Sachems with nine Belts. It is true we are now under much Uneasiness in having trusted so many Sachems in the French Hands, being almost half the Number we have in our Nation, but we were in haste to prevent the Designs the French had against our Countries and yours, by the great warlike Preparations they were making in Canada."

Then he told all the Orders and Directions which their Ambassadors had received; which agreeing with the Account which Decanesora gave of his Negotiation, I shall here pass over. He finished all by giving a Belt.

Colonel Fletcher told them, he would give no Answer to what they had said, before they discovered to him what Reason they had to say, that he had forbid their holding any Assembly at Onondaga, and that he had made Peace with the Dewagunhas and Satanas, without their Consent and Concurrence.

To this the Speaker the next Day answered; "I was sick, and absent when the Affairs you mention were transacted, and I was at a Loss how to excuse our sending to the French contrary to your Advice; but several Sachems being arrived since I spoke, I have been better informed by them, who were present at those Transactions. We find it, in every Circumstance, as our Brother Cayenguirago says; that you did not obstruct our keeping General Councils at Onondaga, but only cautioned us in hearkening to the Fallacies of the French, and in holding Meetings on that Occasion. We assure you we will never separate from you, we still have one Head, one Blood, one Soul, and one Heart with you; and as a Confirmation of this I give this Belt seven deep.

"As to the Dewagunhas and Shawonons, we are confident Cayenguirago will not admit them into his Government, till they have made Peace with us, which we shall willingly grant. When our Enemies are humbled, and beg Peace, why should they not have it? Let them come and live with us, it will strengthen our Country.

"Brother Cayenguirago, when the Christians first arrived in this Country, we received them kindly. When they were but a small People, we entered into a League with them, to guard them from all Enemies whatsoever. We were so fond of their Society, that we tied the great Canoe which brought them, not with a Rope made of Bark to a Tree, but with a strong iron Chain fastened to a great Mountain. Now before the

Christians arrived, the General Council of the Five Nations was held at Onondaga, where there has, from the Beginning, a continual Fire been kept burning; it is made of two great Logs, whose Fire never extinguishes. As soon as the Hatchet-makers (their general Name for Christians) arrived, this General Council at Onondaga planted this Tree at Albany, whose Roots and Branches have since spread as far as New-England, Connecticut, Pensilvania, Maryland and Virginia; and under the Shade of this Tree all these English Colonies have frequently been sheltered. Then (giving seven Fathom of Wampum) he renewed the Chain, and promised, as they likewise expected, mutual Assistance, in Case of any Attack from any Enemy.

"The only Reason, to be plain with you, continued he, of our sending to make Peace with the French, is the low Condition to which we are reduced, while none of our Neighbours send us the least Assistance, so that the whole Burthen of the War lyes on us alone. Our Brethren of New-England, Connecticut, Pensilvania, Maryland and Virginia, of their own accord thrust their Arms into our Chain; but since the War began we have received no Assistance from them. We alone cannot continue the War against the French, by Reason of the Recruits they daily receive from the other Side the great Lake.

"Brother Cayenguirago, speak from your Heart, are you resolved to prosecute the War vigorously against the French, and are your Neighbours of Virginia, Maryland, Pensilvania, Connecticut and New-England, resolved to assist us? If it be so, we assure you, notwithstanding any Treaty hitherto entered into, we will prosecute the War as hotly as ever. But if our Neighbours will not assist, we must make Peace, and we submit it to your Consideration, by giving this great Belt fifteen deep.

"Brother Cayenguirago, I have truly told you the Reasons which have induced us to offer Peace to the French; we shall likewise, from the Bottom of our Hearts, inform you of the Design we have in this Treaty. When the Governor of Canada shall have accepted the nine Belts, of which I have just now told you, then we shall have something more to say by two large Belts, which lye still hid in our Bosom. We shall lay down first one and say, We have a Brother Cayenguirago, with whose People we have been united in one Chain from the Beginning, they must be included in this Treaty; we cannot see them involved in bloody War, while we sit in easy Peace. If the Governor of Canada answer, that he has made a separate Peace with us, and that he cannot make any Peace with Cayenguirago, because the War is from over the great Lake; then we shall lay down the second great broad Belt, and tell the Governor of Canada, if you will not include Cayenguirago's People, the Treaty will become thereby void, as if it had never been made; and if he persists, we will absolutely leave him."

While the Sachems were at Albany, Decanesora and the other Ambassadors arrived at the Castle of the Praying Indians, near the Falls above Montreal. They were conducted from thence, by the Superior of the Jesuits, to Quebeck. They had their Audience of the Governor of Canada with great Solemnity, in the Presence of all the Ecclesiasticks and Officers of Distinction, and of the most considerable Indians then in the Place. They were every Day, while they staid in the Place, entertained at the Governor's Table, or at the Tables of the most considerable Officers. Decanesora on his Side made a good Appearance, being cloathed in Scarlet trim'd with Gold, and with a laced Bever Hat on his Head, which had been given him by Colonel Fletcher before he went.

The Jesuit Milet had by Letter informed the Governor of every Thing in their Commission, and though he was thereby enabled to have answered them immediately, he consulted three Days, after the Ambassadors had delivered what they had to say, before he would return an Answer, that it might appear with more Solemnity. The Indians never return a sudden Answer on any Occasion of Importance, however resolved they be beforehand, and despise those that do, though their Answer be never so much to the Purpose. I choose to give an Account of this from Decanesora's Mouth, as I did of the former, and for the same Reason. The Account given of it by the Indians agrees, in all the material Points, with that published by the French, and I am confident it is not less genuine.

Colonel Fletcher being sensible of what Consequence this Treaty between the French and Five Nations might be of to all the English Colonies, gave them Notice of it, and informed them of the Reasons which had induced the Indians to enter into it. He told them, there was no Possibility of preventing it, but by the Indians being assured of more effectual Assistance, than they had hitherto received, and advised them to send Commissioners for that Purpose to Albany in August, at which Time he intended to meet the Five Nations there, after the Return of their Messengers from Canada. Accordingly, Andrew Hamilton, Esq; Governor of New-Jersey, Colonel John Pinchon, Samuel Sands, Esq; and Major Pen Townsend, Commissioners from Massachuset's Bay, and Colonel John Hauley and Captain Stanley, Commissioners from Connecticut, waited on Colonel Fletcher at Albany, who carried with him likewise a Part of the Council of New-York.

These Gentlemen having met the Indians at Albany the fifteenth of August, Decanesora rose up first, and desired Leave to sing a Song or two of Peace, before they began on Business. Then Rode, a Mohawk Sachem, rose up, and addressing himself to the other Sachems, said, we have great Reason to rejoice, seeing so many of those, who are in our Chain, are now met, to consult together on the general Weal; after which they sang two or three Songs.

Sadakanahtie being chosen Speaker for that Day, rose up, spoke much to the same Purpose as he had done to Colonel Fletcher in May last; giving a metaphorical Account of their League with the English, how it began, and by what Steps it had been inlarged and strengthened; how the other Colonies had thrust their Arms into this Chain, but had given little or no Assistance against the common Enemy. "Our Brother Cayenguirago's Arms (says he) and ours are stiff, and tired with holding fast the Chain, whilst our Neighbours sit still and smoak at their Ease. The Fat is melted from our Flesh, and fallen on our Neighbours, who grow fat while we grow lean: They flourish while we decay.

"This Chain made us the Envy of the French, and if all had held it as fast as Cayenguirago, it would have been a Terror also. If we would all heartily join and take the Hatchet in our Hand, our common Enemy would soon be destroyed, and we should for ever after live in Peace and Ease. Do you but your Parts, and Thunder itself cannot break our Chain."

Then he mentioned some Jealousies they had entertained of New-England, by their suffering the Chevalier D'O to escape to Canada, which they suspected had been concerted between him and the People of New-England, in Order to treat of Peace. "Our Agents, said he, saw the Chevalier D'O at Canada, who told them that he had been set at Liberty by the English, and that it was in vain that the Five Nations warred against the French, while the English favoured them." On this Occasion he shewed them a Fish painted on Paper, which the Commissioners of New-England had given them, when they first entered into the Chain, as a Seal to the League.

He finished by telling them, that they would next Day give all the Particulars of their Negotiation in Canada.

The next Day Decanesora proceeded to the Account of his Negotiation, as follows: "The Governor of Canada having often sent to us to come to Canada to treat with him, we went thither, and told him that we were come to treat of Peace. We made the following Proposals.

"Father, if we do not conclude a Peace now, it will be your Fault; for we have already taken the Hatchet out of the Hands of the River Indians (Hudson's River) whom we incited to the War. But we must tell you, that you are an ill Man, you are inconstant and not to be trusted; we have had War together a long Time, and though you occasioned the War, we never hated the House of Oghessa, (a Gentleman living at Montreal) let him undertake the toilsome Journey to Onondaga; for if he will he shall be welcome.

"Father, we are now speaking of Peace, and therefore I must speak a Word to the Praying Indians, and first to those of Cahnaaga (chiefly Mohawks) you know our Customs and Manners, therefore make Onondio acquainted therewith, and be assisting in the prosecuting of this good Work. Then to the other Castle, called Canassadaga, (chiefly Onondagas) you are worse than the French themselves, you deserted from us, and side with our Enemies to destroy us; make some amends now, by forwarding Peace.

"You have almost eat us up, our best Men are killed in this bloody War; but we now forget what is past. Before this we once threw the Hatchet into the River of Kaihohage,* but you fished it up, and treacherously surprised our People at Cadarackui. After this you sent to us to have our Prisoners restored; then the Hatchet was thrown up to the Sky, but you kept a String fastened to the Helve, and pulled it down, and fell upon our People again. This we revenged to some Purpose, by the Destruction of your People and Houses in the Island of Montreal.

"Now we are come to cover the Blood from our Sight, which has been shed by both Sides during this long War.

"Onondio, we have been at War a long Time, we now give you a Medicine to drive away all ill Thoughts from your Heart, to purge it and make it clean, and restore it to its former State.

"Onondio, we will not permit any Settlement at Cadarackui; you have had your Fire there thrice extinguished; we will not consent to your rebuilding that Fort, but the Passage through the River shall be free and clear. We make the Sun clean, and drive away all Clouds and Darkness, that we may see the Light without Interruption.

---

* The French call it la Famine, near Ohswego. The Treaty with Mr. de la Bar was made there.

"Onondio, we have taken many Prisoners from one another, during the War. The Prisoners we took have been delivered, according to our Custom, to the Families that have lost any in the War. They no longer belong to the Publick, they may give them back if they please, your People may do the same. We have brought back two Prisoners, and restore them to you.

"After I had finished what I had to say, continued he, the Governor of Canada told me, that he would not make Peace with Cayenguirago. To this I answered, these Words displease me much, you shall keep Peace with him. Onondio said again, I must fight with Cayenguirago, it is not in my Power to make Peace; this can only be done by my Master, who lives over the great Water. To this I replied, I cannot bear this Discourse; if you should fight him now, and not stay till I get Home, all the Country will look on me as a Traytor; I can treat with you no longer. The Argument on this Subject lasted three Days, at last the Governor of Canada assured me, that he would not undertake any Enterprize against Cayenguirago this Summer, but would wait to hear what he wou'd say.

"The Governor of Canada insisted three Days to have Hostages left, which I refused, but two agreeing of their own accord to stay, they were left, *viz.* one an Onondago, another a Seneka.

"Then the Governor of Canada made the following publick Answer:

"I. I accept of Peace as you offer.

"II. Son, bring all the Prisoners back that you have taken from me, and yours shall have Liberty to return Home, if they please.

"III. Children, erect my Fire again at Cadarackui, and plant there the Tree of Peace.

"After this the Governor of Canada delivered me a Belt, which I now lay down before you; by it he said, desire Cayenguirago to send a wise Man to me, and he shall have

Protection according to the Custom of Christians; and added,

"Children of the Five Nations, if Cayenguirago shall employ you to do any Service for him, do not accept of it, let him send his own People." Decanesora added, that the Governor of Canada had fixed eighty Days for a Return to this Belt.

He continued and said, "The Sachems of the Dionondadies were present; after I had finished my Speech, they said; May what you have now said be from your Hearts; we suspect you are not sincere; let us no longer feel the Smart of the Hatchet, and gave this Belt which I now lay down.

"The Praying Indians next said, Brethren, our Father Onondio has told you to bring Home all the Prisoners, do not fail in this; giving two Belts.

"Brother Cayenguirago, you will find what I have now said confirmed by this Paper, which the Governor of Canada gave me. I brought Letters likewise for the Jesuit Milet, who was to read the Paper to us." The Paper contained the Articles in French, in which the Governor of Canada was willing to make Peace.

But besides what Decanesora here tells, the French Accounts say, that he brought two Belts underground (that is privately) from three Onondaga Sachems, to assure the Governor of Canada of their particular Affection, which the Governor of Canada answered, by a private Belt to them.

As soon as Decanesora had done speaking, Colonel Fletcher rejected the Belt sent by the Governor of Canada, saying; If the Governor of Canada have any Thing to say to me, let him send some of his People to Albany, and they shall have Protection.

Next Day Sadekanahtie, after he had sung a long Song, gave the following Account of their Negotiations with the Dewagunhas and Dionondadies, which they had undertaken by the Governor's Advice.

"We were afraid, says he, to send Messengers of our own People, and therefore we employed two Prisoners we had of the Dionondadies with the Governor's Belt. Some time after this, some of the Senekas hunting near the Dionondadies, two of them were taken; but when they were carried to the Dionondadie Castle, they were not treated like Prisoners; they were used kindly, and sent back with the following Offers of Peace.

"We are glad to see you Face to Face to speak to you, since the Sun has been so propitious to send home the men that were Prisoners with you, giving a few Strings of Wampum.

"We are glad of this Opportunity to tell you, that we have been both drunk in making War on one another; we now give you a Cordial to ease your Hearts, that there be no longer War between us, by this Belt.

"We are glad that you have set the Doors open as far as Cayenguirago's House, that we may freely go thither. Carry him this second Belt.

"Brethren, we thank you for having prepared a Place for us at your General Council of Onondaga. Our Country is every where free to you to treat with us, by this third Belt.

"Brethren, our whole Country rejoiced when you invited us into your Country, and from thence to go where Cayenguirago dwells; be not afraid to come to our Country, you shall meet with no Molestation.

"Brethren, we thank you for putting us in Mind of what was formerly agreed to, *viz.* that when any ill Accident happens, we were to meet together to compose Matters, and not to revenge it with War. We are now together to put an End to all Misunderstanding, by this fourth Belt.

"Brethren, (we include all the Nations from the Senekas Country to New-York in this Name) hearken to us. We rend the Clouds asunder, and drive away all Darkness from the Heavens, that the Sun of Peace may shine with Brightness over us all; giving a Sun of a round red polished Stone.

"Brethren, we put the Hatchet into the Hands of the Chightaghies, Twithtwies, and Odsirachies, to war against you; but we shall in three Days go to these Nations and take the Hatchet out of their Hands; giving half a Stone Pipe.

"You Senekas are stupid Creatures, we must therefore warn

you not to hunt so far from your Castles, lest you be hurt by any of these three Nations, and then blame us. They then gave the other half of the Pipe.

"But Brother Cayenguirago, says Sadakahnitie, do not suffer these Nations to come nearer than the Senekas Country, lest they discover our Weakness, and to what a low Condition the War has reduced us. These Nations have been so long in Friendship with the French, and are so much under their Influence, that we cannot trust them yet, or be too much upon our Guard against them."

Colonel Fletcher not being able to give the Five Nations any Assurance of a vigorous Assistance, he called the principal Sachems to a private Conference on the twentieth. He asked them, whether they had made Peace with the Governor of Canada; they answered, that it only wanted his Approbation, and added, that they could no longer carry on the War without Assistance. You have the whole Negotiations before you, say they, and we submit it to your Prudence.

He then allowed them to make Peace, provided they kept faithful in their Chain with the English; but told them, that as to his Part he could make no Peace with the Governor of Canada. They were under great Uneasiness to leave their Friends in the War, they said, and wished, since neither the Governor of Canada nor he would receive Proposals by their Hands, that they might think of some neutral Place to treat. The Governor answered, that he could neither receive nor send any Message on that Head; and that Peace could be only made between them by the two Kings.

The Governor next asked them, whether they would permit the French to build again at Cadarackui; they answered, they would never permit it, and were resolved to insist on it, in all the ensuing Treaties, that he never shall. Then the Governor added, if you permit the French to build any where on that Lake, there will be an End to your Liberty, your Posterity will become Slaves to the French. If ever you should permit them, I will look on it as an absolute Breach of the Chain with us: If the French attempt it give me Notice, and I will march the whole Force of my Government to your Assistance. We shall find afterwards, however, that the Government of New-York was far from making good this Promise.

The Governor told them, that they had lost much of their Honour in creeping to the French, in such an abject Manner; for, says he, the Governor of Canada's Paper, which you brought with you, says, that you came in the most humble and penitent Manner, and begged Peace. To which they answered, the Governor of Canada has no Reason to make such Reflexions, we have many of his Belts to shew, by which he again and again sued to us for Peace, before we would hearken to him. But, replies the Governor, how came you to call him Father? For no other Reason, they replied, but because he calls us Children. These Names signify nothing.

They desired the Governor not to say any Thing particularly of Cadarackui, in his publick Speech that he was to make next Day, for they had, they said, some among them that would tell all to the Governor of Canada; and concluded, with wishing that they had some one, who could write and read all that the Governor had said to them, that they might not forget any Part of it, when they come to consult and resolve on this weighty Affair, at their General Council at Onondaga.

Here we see these Barbarians, these Savages, as we call them, acting with the greatest regard to the Treaties they had entered into with their Allies, and that at a Time when the Exigences of their own Affairs, and when the faint feeble Assistance, which their Allies had contributed in the common Cause, would, among Christian Potentates, have been thought a sufficient Excuse for their taking Care of themselves separately, in breach of the most solemn Confederacy they could enter into.

The Sachems of the Five Nations being met at Onondaga, to consult on the Terms offered by the French, they were divided in their Opinions; the Cayugas, and Part of the Senekas, were most favorable to the French Proposals; but the major Part was absolutely against allowing the French to rebuild a Fort at Cadarackui, nor would they consent to include all the French Allies in the Treaty, with some of which they had particular Causes of Animosity.

The Party that was most for Peace obtained Leave to go to Canada, to try whether they could obtain Terms less disagreeable. They accordingly went thither, within the Time prefixed by the Governor of Canada, for an Answer; and to make themselves more acceptable to the French, they carried thirteen Prisoners with them, and delivered them up. The Jesuit Milet was of this Number, who had been taken in the Year 1689, and one Jonscaire, who had been long a Prisoner among the Senekas: He had been delivered up to a Family of the Senekas, that had lost some considerable Relation, and was by them adopted. He ingratiated himself so much with that Nation, that he was advanced to the Rank of a Sachem, and preserved their Esteem to the Day of his Death; whereby he became, after the general Peace, very useful to the French in all Negotiations with the Five Nations, and to this Day they shew their Regard to his Family and Children.

When the Governor of Canada came to Particulars with these Deputies, he could obtain nothing but ambiguous or dubious Answers, as to the rebuilding of Cadarackui Fort, and the including of all the French Allies in the Peace. Whereupon he dismissed them with Presents, and made them many fair Promises, in Case of their Compliance; but threatened them with utter Destruction, in Case of their refusing the Terms he had offered. Many of the French Indian Allies were present, when the Governor of Canada refused any Agreement without his Allies being included in it, and this attached them exceedingly to the French Interest. This Regard, which the French generally shew for the Interest of their Allies, is a Piece of Policy which, upon all Occasions, proves useful to them; whereas, the Neglect of this Piece of natural Justice has as often been prejudicial to others, who have not had so tender a Sense of it. But it is not so easy for a weak State to keep up its Honour in such Cases, as it is for a powerful Prince.

CHAP. XI.

The War renewed. The French repossess them-selves of Cadarackui Fort, and find Means to break off the Treaty between the Five Nations and Dionondadies.

THE Five Nations refusing to come to the Governor of Canada's Terms, he resolved to force them; and as he suspected that they continued obstinate, by the Advice of the English, and the Confidence they had of the English Assistance, he thought he would most effectually lessen that Confidence, by attacking and destroying the remainder of the Mohawks, who liv'd adjoining to the English Settlements. For this Purpose he resolved to march, in the Winter, the whole Force of Canada against that Nation; but one of the Prisoners learning their Design, made his Escape, and informed the Mohawks of it. This made him alter his Measures, knowing well enough, that if the English were prepared to receive them, such an Enterprize would only lead those engaged in it to certain Destruction. He then sent three hundred Men into the Neck of Land between Lake Erie and Cadarackui Lake, the usual hunting Place of the Five Nations, in hopes of surprising them while they hunted carelessly there, and at the same Time to view the old French Fort there, to observe in what Condition it remained.

This Party met with three or four Men, who defended themselves obstinately, till they all fell dead on the Spot. They surprised likewise a Cabin, where they took some Men and Women Prisoners; and four of them were publickly burnt alive at Montreal. So far the Count de Frontenac thought it more proper to imitate the Indians in their most savage Cruelties, than to instruct them, by his Example, in the Compassion of the Christian Doctrine. A Party of one hundred and fifty of the Five Nations fell upon the Dewagunhas, in their Way to Canada, and entirely routed them. Ten Prisoners were taken, nine of which were burnt alive, in revenge of the same Fate the four Men of the Five Nations had received at Montreal.

This Year also some sculking French Indians murdered some People near Albany and Schenectady.

The Party sent to view Cadarackui Fort found it in a better Condition than they expected, the Indians having neglected to demolish and level the Bastions, and probably they had not Instruments sufficient to do it. The Count de Frontenac therefore, in the Summer of the Year 1695, sent a considerable Body of Men, both French and Indians, thither, to repair the Fortifications, and to cover those that should be at work. The Five Nations, in August, sent Messengers to Albany, to acquaint the English that the French had taken Possession of Cadarackui, and were repairing of it. They demanded, in Consequence of the Promise Colonel Fletcher had given them, the Assistance of five hundred Men and some Canon, which they promised they would draw over Land, where they could not be carried by Water. At the same Time they desired, that the People of New-England might be told, that many of the Owenagungas were gone with the French to Cadarackui, and that this was a proper Time to fall upon those that remained, and to destroy them, and the Women and Children.

Coll. Fletcher came to Albany in September; there, in a Speech to the Five Nations, he blamed them for being asleep, when they suffered the French to take Possession of Cadarackui; it would have been much easier, he said, to have prevented their getting the Possession, than to drive them out, now they are in it, especially as now you yourselves are convinced, that it is impossible to carry Cannon thither from this Place. All, says he, I can now do, is to advise you to invest the Place with your Parties, so as to prevent their receiving any Supply of Provisions: By this Means you may force them to desert it. Then he gave them 1000 Pound of Powder, two Thousand Pound of Lead, 57 Fusees, one Hundred Hatchets, three Hundred and forty eight Knives, and two Thousand Flints, besides Cloathing, &c. But in my Opinion, the Government of New-York have, on all Occasions, been exceedingly to be blamed, in not having some Men of Experience among the Five Nations to advise and direct them on all Emergencies of Importance. The French are very careful of this, and the Officers of the regular Troops are obliged to take their Tours among their Indians, while the Captains of the independent Companies of Fusiliers at New-York live like military Monks, in Idleness and Luxury.

The French gained a great Advantage, by possessing this Place, as it is of great Security to their Traders, in their passing between Montreal and Missilimakinak. It served likewise as a Place of Stores, and Retreat in all their Enterprises against the Five Nations, that Place being nearly about half Way between Montreal and the Country of the Five Nations. It likewise exposed the Five Nations in their hunting, to the Incursions of that Garison, by its being in the Neighbourhood of their principal hunting Place for Bever.

The French grew exceedingly uneasy, when they found, that the Dionondadies, who live near Missilimakinak, had almost concluded a Peace with the Five Nations, and that the rest of their Allies were like to follow their Example: Some of these Nations had been at Montreal, and at their Return forwarded the Peace, that thereby they might be at Liberty to go to Albany; for they informed their Neighbours, that the Five Nations had intirely shut up the Path to Montreal; and besides that, the French were not in a Condition to supply them, for they had nothing for themselves, not so much as a Drop of strong Spirits. If these Nations had, at that Time, deserted the French, it might probably have put an End to the French Colony; for as the Lands of Canada barely produce sufficient for the Subsistence of its Inhabitants, the only Means they have of purchasing Cloathing and other Necessaries is by their Trade with the Indians. The French likewise had been in Danger of greater Mischief by the Peace, for these Nations being at War with the Five Nations, and lying on the Back of them, obliged the Five Nations to keep always a very considerable Part of their Force at home, to defend themselves against these Nations, and to revenge the Injuries they received from them; but if the Peace had been concluded with these Nations, the Five Nations could have turned their whole Force against Canada, and probably might have persuaded these Nations to have joined with them in warring on the French.

The French Commandant at Missilimakinak had his Hands full at this Time; and if he had not been a Man of great Abilities, he must have sunk under the Difficulties he had to go through; in the first Place, to contradict the Stories brought from Montreal, he ordered the Stores of his Fort to be sold to the Indians at the cheapest Rate, and assured them, that great Quantities were every Day expected from France, which were only detained by contrary Winds; and after these Goods shall arrive, said he, they will be sold cheaper than ever they have been. He told them likewise, that the Count de Frontenac would never make Peace with the Five Nations, but was resolved to extirpate them; for which Purpose he was now rebuilding Cadarackui Fort. At the same Time he took all possible Methods to extinguish the Beginnings of Friendship, which appeared between the Five Nations and Dionondadies.

The Dionondadies durst not avow their treating with the Five Nations to the French, neither durst the Five Nations trust their Agents in a Place where they knew the French had so great Influence; both Sides therefore agreed to carry on their Treaty by Means of Prisoners which they took from one another. The Civility with which the Dionondadies treated these Prisoners, their dismissing them, and their receiving again Prisoners which had been taken by the Five Nations, gave the Commandant sufficient Ground to suspect what was doing. The Dionondadies at last took seven Men of the Five Nations Prisoners, and carried them to Missilimakinak. The French perceiving, by their Manner of bringing them in, that the Dionondadies intended to treat them with the Civility they had lately used to others, murdered two of them with their Knives as they stept ashore. On this the Dionondadies immediately took to their Arms, saved the other Five, and carried them safe to their Castle; and continuing in Arms, threatened Revenge for the Insult they had received.

The French were forced in like Manner to stand to their Arms, and as there are always many different Nations at Missilimakinak trading, some of which were inveterate Enemies of the Five Nations, they joined with the French. The Utawawas stood neuter. This gave the Commandant Means of ending the Dispute by Composition. He in the first Place assured them, that the Christians abhorred all Manner of Cruelty, and then told them, that as the French shared with the Dionondadies in all the Dangers and Losses sustained by the War, they ought in like Manner to partake with them in any Advantage. The Dionondadies on this were persuaded to deliver up one of the Prisoners. What I am about to relate, I think, gives Room to charge the French with a Piece of Policy, not only inconsistent with the Christian Religion, but likewise with the Character of a polite People; and that all Considerations from Religion, Honour, and Virtue, must give Way to the present Exigencies of their Affairs. That an End might be put to the Beginnings of a Reconciliation between these People and the Five Nations, the French gave a publick Invitation to feast on the Soup to be made on this Prisoner, and, in a more particular Manner, invited the Utawawas to the Entertainment.

The Prisoner being first made fast to a Stake, so as to have Room to move round it, a Frenchman began the horrid Tragedy, by broiling the Flesh of the Prisoner's Legs, from his Toes to his Knees, with the red hot Barrel of a Gun; his Example was followed by an Utawawa, and they relieved one another as they grew tired. The Prisoner all this while continued his Death Song, till they clapt a red hot Frying-pan on his Buttocks, when he cried out, Fire is strong and too powerful; then all their Indians mocked him, as wanting Courage and Resolution. You, they said, a Soldier and a Captain, as you say, and afraid of Fire; you are not a Man. They continued their Torments for two Hours without ceasing. An Utawawa being desirous to outdo the French in their refined Cruelty, split a Furrow from the Prisoner's Shoulder to his Garter, and filling it with Gunpowder, set Fire to it. This gave him exquisite Pain, and raised excessive Laughter in his Tormenters. When they found his Throat so much parched, that he was no longer able to gratify their Ears with his howling, they gave him Water, to enable him to continue their Pleasure longer. But at last his Strength failing, an Utawawa flead off his Scalp, and threw burning hot Coals on his Scull. Then they untied him, and bid him run for his Life: He began to run, tumbling like a drunken Man; they shut up the Way to the East, and made him run Westward, the Country, as they think, of departed (miserable) Souls. He had still Force left to throw Stones, till they put an End to his Misery by knocking him on the Head with a Stone. After this every one cut a Slice from his Body, to conclude the Tragedy with a Feast. It is doing no Injury, I think, to these Frenchmen, who thus glory in this horrid Cruelty, to ask them, whether they did not likewise regale their revengeful Appetites with a Share of this inhuman Feast?

Though I have had frequent Occasions to mention these barbarous inhuman Cruelties, transacted by the Indians, yet I have avoided to relate the particular Circumstances of them, because I believe few civilized Ears can bear the reading of them without Horror. But when they are perpetrated by Christians, and so far gloried in, as to be recorded in their own History, I am willing to shew it to my Countrymen in its proper Colours. This last Piece of French History is taken from *Histoire de l'Amerique Septentrionale, par Monsr. de la Poterie,* published at Paris with the Royal Licence, and recommended to the Publick by Mons. Fontenelle, Vol. ii. Page 298.

Though this cruel Act had its designed Effect, in breaking off this Method of negotiating between the Five Nations and Dionondadies, it did not prevent the Peace; and it had very near raised a Civil War with their own Indians, which was only prevented by the dextrous Conduct of the French Officers, who, in all kind of Artifice, have always been superior to the Indians. But let me observe on this Occasion, that the avoiding any Misfortune, by any base or wicked Action, is commonly the Cause of greater Mischiefs than what is thereby avoided; and of this numerous Examples may be given.

CHAP. XII.

The Count de Frontenac attacks Onondaga in Person, with the whole Force of Canada. The Five Nations continue the War with the French, and make Peace with the Dionondadies.

THE Count de Frontenac having secured Cadarackui Fort, which was called by his Name, as a Place of Arms and Provisions, and for a Retreat to the Men that should happen to be sick or wounded, resolved to make the Five Nations feel his Resentment of their refusing his Terms of Peace. For this Purpose he assembled all the regular Troops of Canada, the Militia, the Owenagungas, the Quatoghies of Loretto, the Adirondacks, Sokokies, Nepiciriniens, the Praying Indians of the Five Nations, and a few Utawawas, at Montreal, in June

1696. The other western Indians near Missilimakinak, by their late Correspondence with the Five Nations, and the Dissatisfaction they had manifested, were not trusted. The Manner of making War with the Indians in a Country wholly covered with Woods, must be so much different from the Methods used in Europe, that I believe the Reader will be pleased to have a particular Account of the Count de Frontenac's Conduct in this, who was an old experienced General, in the seventy fourth Year of his Age.

It is to be observed, that it is impossible to pass the vast Forests between the Countries of the Five Nations with Waggons, or other Carriages, or on Horseback, or even on Foot, in the summer Time, by Reason of many impassible thick Swamps and Morasses. For this Reason, the only Method of travelling is in Bark Canoes, or very light Battoes, along the Rivers, which may be easily carried on Men's Shoulders, where the Stream of the River becomes too rapid, and from one River to another; for which Purpose the shortest Passes are always chosen, and are called, for this Reason, Carrying Places.

The Count de Frontenac marched from la Chine, in the south End of the Island of Montreal, the fourth of July. He divided five hundred Indians so, that the greatest Number of them should always be in the Van, which consisted of two Battalions of the regular Troops. They were followed by the Canoes which carried the Provisions. The Van was commanded by the Chevalier de Callieres, Governor of Montreal; he had with him two large Battoes, which carried two small Pieces of Cannon, small Mortars, Granadoes, and the Utensils of the Artillery. The Count de Frontenac was at the Head of the main Body, accompanied by the Engineer and several Gentlemen Voluntiers. The Body consisted of four Battalions of the Militia, who, in War with Indians, were then more depended on than the regular Troops; these were commanded by Monsieur Ramsay, Governor of Trois Rivieres. The Rear, which consisted of two Battalions of regular Troops, and of the rest of the Indians, was under the Command of the Chevalier de Vaudreuil. All the Indians had French Officers set over them.

In this Order the Army marched, only those that were in the Van one Day, were in the Rear the next; and they always kept a Number of Indians on the Scout, to discover the Tracks of the Enemy, for fear of Ambuscades. And when they were obliged to carry the Canoes, and drag the large Battoes, several Parties were detached to cover the Men that worked.

After twelve Days March they arrived at Cadarackui Fort, one hundred eighty Miles from Montreal. Here they waited for the Utawawas, who disappointed them; and in the mean Time raised a Bark, which had remained sunk since Cadarackui Fort was deserted. They crossed over Cadarackui Lake to Onondaga River (now Ohswega). This River being narrow and rapid, they ordered fifty Men to march on each Side of it, to prevent their being surprised, and the Army moved slowly along the River, according to the Intelligence they received from their scouts. They found a Tree, as they passed along, on which the Indians had, in their Manner, painted the French Army, and had laid by it two Bundles of cut Rushes. This was a Defiance in the Indian Manner, and to tell them by the Number of Rushes, that fourteen hundred thirty four Men would meet them. The French passed the little Lake, between Ohswega and Onondaga, in Order of Battle; and the two Wings, to prevent their being surprised, and to make the Place of their Landing more uncertain to the Enemy, took a Circuit along the Coast. As soon as they had landed they raised a Fort. A Seneka, who had been some time a Prisoner in Canada, and pretended an Attachment to the French, was sent out to make a Discovery. He deserted to the Onondagas. He found them waiting for the French, with a Resolution to defend their Castle, and to fight the French; for which Purpose they had sent away their Women and Children. The Seneka told them that the French Army was as numerous as the Leaves on the Trees; that they had Machines which threw

Balls up in the Air, and which falling on their Castle burst to Pieces, and spread Fire and Death every where, against which their Stockadoes could be of no Defence. This was confirmed by another Seneka, who deserted. Upon which the Onondagas thought it most adviseable to retire, leaving their poor Fort and bark Cottages all in Flames.

After the General had an Account of this, he marched to their Village in Order of Battle. The Army was divided into two Lines: The first commanded by the Chevalier de Callieres, who placed himself on the Left, consisted of two Battalions of the Inhabitants in the Center, and a Battalion of the regular Troops on each Wing. The Artillery followed them. Most of the Indians of this Division were upon the Right, who continually sent out Scouts. The second Line was commanded by the Chevalier de Vaudreuel, composed of the same Number of Battalions, and in the same Order. The Count de Frontenac was carried in a Chair directly after the Artillery. But it was impossible for them to keep their Order, in passing through thick Woods, and in passing Brooks. In this formidable Manner the aged General marched up to the Ashes of the Village, and his Army exerted their Fury on the Indian Corn, which covered a large Field in thick Ranks.

An Indian Sachem, about one hundred Years old, would not retire with the rest, but chose this Time to end his Days. The French Indians had the Pleasure of tormenting him, which he bore with surprising Evenness of Mind, and with that Resolution which becomes a Sachem of the Five Nations. He told his Tormentors to remember well his Death, when his Countrymen should come to take terrible Vengeance of them. Upon which, one stabbing him several Times with his Knife, he thanked him but said, you had better make me die by Fire, that these Dogs of Frenchmen may learn how to suffer like Men. You Indians, their Allies, you Dogs of Dogs, think of me when you shall be in the like State. Thus this old Sachem, under all the Weakness of old Age, preserved a Greatness of Soul, and a due Regard for the Honour of his Country, to the last Moment of his Breath.

The Chevalier de Vaudreuil was sent with a Detachment of six or seven hundred Men to destroy the Oneydoes Corn, who liv'd but a small Distance from Onondaga, which he performed without any Resistance. The Jesuit Milet had lived for the most Part with the Oneydoes; he had infused into them the most favourable Sentiments of the French, and they had been the most inclined to Peace on the French Terms. Thirty five of them staid in their Castle to make the French welcome; but the only Favour they obtained, was to be made Prisoners, and carried to Montreal. The French Governor declared his Resolutions to extirpate the Onondagas, and for that Reason gave Orders to give no Quarter.

The Difficulty of supporting so many Men in these Deserts, made it necessary for the Count de Frontenac to return as speedily as possible. Though the French Army was much an Overmatch for the Onondagas, both in Number of Men and in their Arms, the Onondagas were not so far dispirited, as not to follow them in their Return. They found Opportunities to revenge themselves in some Measure, by cutting off every Canoe that happened at any Time to be at a Distance from the main Body. This obliged the Count to hasten his March, so that he returned to Montreal the tenth of August.

The Onondagas suffered nothing by this chargeable Expedition, but the Loss of their Corn, and their Bark Cottages. They lost not one Man, but the old Sachem, who resolved to die a Martyr to his Country's Honour. The French suffered considerably by its Consequences; for all the Planters being taken off from their Labour, either in this Expedition, or in watching and securing their Forts and Country, a Famine ensued; and this I find has often happened in Canada, where all the Men, fit to bear Arms, have been employed in such like Expeditions. If the Oneydoes had not timely surrendered themselves, the Count had not been able to have carried Home the

least Token of a Victory. And all that can be said for this Enterprize is, that it was a kind of heroick Dotage.

The Influence that the Jesuit Milet had obtained over the
Oneydoes was such, that some Time after this, thirty of them
deserted to the French, and desired that he might be appointed their Pastor.

In the following Winter the Mohawks, with the Governor
of New-York's Privacy, sent one to the Praying Indians with
two Belts, and he carried two Prisoners with him. By the first
Belt he asked, whether the Path was entirely shut up between
their two Countries; and, by the second, demanded the
Restitution of a Prisoner the Praying Indians had taken: But
his real Design was, to learn the State of their Country, and
what Designs were forming. Notwithstanding the Influence
and Artifice of the French Priests over these Converts, they
still retained an Affection to their Countrymen; for which
Reason the Count de Frontenac entertained a Jealousy of
these Intercourses, and threatened to put to Death any that
should come in that Manner again; but the Messenger had
the Satisfaction of discovering the distressed Condition of
Canada by Famine.

A Party of the French was sent out in the Winter, to make
some Attempt upon the English Settlements near Albany;
but some Mohawks and Scahkook Indians meeting with them,
before they reached the Settlements, they were intirely routed.
The commanding Officer, one du Bau, and two others, saved
themselves from the Fury of the Indians, by running to Albany; the rest were either killed or perished in the Woods,
so that not one Man of this Party got back to Canada.

It was much easier for the French to set the Praying Indians
upon the English, against whom it is possible many of them
had personal Animosities, that made them go over to the
French, than to fight their Countrymen. Several of them came
this Winter skulking about Schenectady and Albany; and
being well acquainted with the Country, and speaking likewise the Mohawk's Language, by which they sometimes de-

ceived the Inhabitants, they surprised some of the Inhabitants, and carried away their Scalps.

The Five Nations, to shew that the Count de Frontenac's Expedition had no Way discouraged them, sent out several Parties against Canada. One of them met with a Party of French upon St. Laurence River, near Montreal. The French were routed, and their Captain killed. As soon as this was heard at Montreal, Repentigni was sent out after them with a considerable Party of French, Nepicirinien Indians and Praying Indians; but this Party was likewise defeated, and the Captain, with many of his Men, killed.

Thus the War was continued till the Peace of Reswick, by small Parties of Indians, on both Sides, harassing, surprising, and scalping the Inhabitants near Montreal and Albany.

Some Time this Year the chief Sachem of the Dionondadies (whom the French call the Baron) went to Quebeck, pretending a strong Attachment to the French, but really to conceal the Treaty of Peace that he was on the Point of concluding with the Five Nations; for which Purpose he had sent his Son with nineteen Belts to the Senekas. The Substance of whose Commission was as follows:

The French have for many Years confounded our Resolutions, and deceived us, but now we are resolved to break all their Artifices, by stopping our Ears. We come now to unite with you, while the French know nothing of the Matter. The Commandant at Missilimakinak has told us many Lies, he has betrayed us, and made us kill one another, but we are firmly resolved never to hearken to him any more. The Peace was accordingly firmly concluded, notwithstanding all the Opposition the French could make. The French Authors say, the only Reason that induced the Dionondadies was, that the English sold them Goods cheaper than the French could.

Some Time before the News of the Peace arrived, the French at Montreal being informed that a Party of the Five Nations were discovered near Corlear's Lake, sent out a Captain with a Party of Soldiers and Indians, who being well experienced in the Manner of making War with Indians, marched through the thickest Woods, and by the least frequented Places, so that he discovered the Enemy, without being discovered. He surprised that Party, killed several, and took one Prisoner. The Utawawas being then trading at Montreal, the Count de Frontenac invited them to a Feast to be made of this Prisoner, and caused him to be burnt publickly alive at Montreal, in the Manner of which I have already given two Accounts from the French Authors.

CHAP. XIII.

The Conduct which the English and French observed, in regard to the Five Nations, immediately after the Peace of Reswick.

SOON after the News of the Peace of Reswick reached New-York, the Governor sent an Express to Canada, to inform the Governor there of it, that Hostilities might cease. The Five Nations having an Account of the Peace earlier than they had it in Canada, took Advantage of it, in hunting Bever near Cadarackui Fort. The Governor of Canada being informed of this, and believing that the Five Nations thought themselves secure by the general Peace, resolved to take his last Revenge of them. For this Purpose he sent a considerable Party of Adirondacks to surprise them, which they did, and killed several, but not without Loss of many of their own Men. The Loss of one of their greatest Captains at that Time gave the Five Nations the greatest Affliction. After he was mortally wounded, he cried out: "Must I, who have made the whole Earth tremble before me, now die by the Hands of Children?" for he despised the Adirondacks.

A Dispute at this Time arose, between the Government of

New-York and Canada, about the French Prisoners which the Five Nations had in their Hands. The Earl of Bellamont, then Governor of New-York, would have the French receive those Prisoners from him, and directed the Five Nations to bring them to Albany for that Purpose. The French, on the other Hand, refused to own the Five Nations as subject to the Crown of Great-Britain, and threatened to continue the War against the Five Nations, if they did not bring the Prisoners to Montreal, and deliver them there. The Count de Frontenac sent some of the Praying Indians with a Message to this Purpose, and to have all the French Allies included in the general Peace.

The Messenger on his Return told the Count, publickly in Presence of several Utawawas, that the Five Nations refused to include several of his Allies, but were resolved to revenge the Injuries they had received. The Utawawas were exceedingly discomposed at hearing this, and the Count, to recover their Spirits, assured them, that he never would make Peace without including all his Allies in it, and without having all their Prisoners restored. At the same Time he made Preparations to attack the Five Nations with the whole Force of Canada.

The Earl of Bellamont being informed of this, sent Captain John Schuyler (of the Militia) to tell the Count, that he had the Interest of the King his Master too much at Heart, to suffer the French to treat the Five Nations like Enemies, after the Conclusion of the general Peace; for which Reason he had ordered them to be on their Guard, and had furnished them with Arms and Ammunition; that he had ordered the Lieutenant-Governor, in Case they were attacked, either by the French or their Allies, to join them with the regular Troops; and that, if he found it necessary, he would raise the whole Force of his Government in their Defence.

This put a Stop to the French Threatening, and both Sides made Complaint to their Masters. The two Kings ordered their respective Governors to be assisting to each other, in making the Peace effectual to both Nations, and to leave the Disputes, as to the Dependency of the Indian Nations, to be determined by Commissioners, to be appointed pursuant to the Treaty of Reswick.

It is exceedingly impolitick, when weaker Potentates, ingaged in a Confederacy against one powerful Prince, leave any Points to be determined after the Conclusion of a Peace; for if they cannot obtain a Concession, while the Confederacy stands and their Force is united, how can a weaker Prince hope to obtain it, when he is left alone to himself, after the Confederacy is dissolved? The French have so often found the Benefit of this Peace of Imprudence, that in all their Treaties they use all the Cajoling, and every Artifice in their Power, to obtain this Advantage, and they seldom miss it.

About the Time of the Conclusion of the Peace at Reswick, the noted Therouet died at Montreal. The French gave him Christian Burial in a pompous Manner, the Priest, that attended him at his Death, having declared that he died a true Christian; for, said the Priest, while I explained to him the Passion of our Saviour, whom the Jews crucified, he cried out; "Oh! had I been there, I would have revenged his Death, and brought away their Scalps."

Soon after the Peace was known at Montreal, three considerable Men of the Praying Indians came to Albany; they had fine laced Coats given them, and were invited to return to their own Country. They answered, that they were young Men, and had not Skill to make a suitable Answer, and had not their ancient Men to consult with; but promised to communicate the Proposals to their old Men, and would bring back an Answer in the Fall. I find nothing more of this in the Register of Indian Affairs, though it might have been of great Consequence had it been pursued to Purpose; but such Matters, where there is not an immediate private Profit, are seldom pursued by the English with that Care and Assiduity, with which they are by the French.

While Captain Schuyler was in Canada, he entered into

some indiscreet Discourse with Monsieur Maricour, for whom the Five Nations had a particular Esteem, and called Stowto-wisse. Captain Schuyler, in asserting the Dependency of the Five Nations on New-York, said, that those Nations were their Slaves. Mr. Maricour told this Discourse to an Onondaga, with all the Aggravations he could, and added, that it was intirely owing to the English that the Peace was not abso-lutely concluded, and that Captain Schuyler prevented their Prisoners being restored, because he would have them sent to Albany, as being Slaves to the English. That the French had no Dispute with the English, but for the Independency of the Five Nations. This indiscreet Conduct of Captain Schuyler was so much resented by the Five Nations, that a Deputation of the most considerable Sachems was sent to Al-bany in June 1699, to complain of it; and they sent at the same Time Deputies to Canada to conclude the Peace, independ-ently of the English. These Deputies that came to Albany were so far convinced that the French had abused them, and how much more it was for their Security to be included in the general Peace with the English, than to have only the French Faith for their Security, that they immediately dispatched a Messenger after their Deputies that were gone to Canada. Though this Messenger reached them too late to stop their Proceeding, it convinced the Deputies so far of its being for their Interest to be joined with the English in the Peace, as they had been in the War, that they insisted that the Ex-change of Prisoners be made at Albany. At the same Time the Messenger was sent after their Deputies to Canada, Colo-nel Peter Schuyler was sent with others to Onondaga, to re-move the Prejudices they had received there.

The Count de Frontenac died while these Disputes con-tinued. Monsieur de Callieres, who succeeded him, put an End to them, by agreeing to send to Onondaga to regulate the Exchange of Prisoners there; for which Purpose Monsieur Maricour, Ioncaire, and the Jesuit Bruyas, were sent.

When the French Commissioners were come within less

than a Mile of Onondaga Castle, they put themselves in Order and marched with the French Colours carried before them, and with as much Show as they could make. Decanesora met them without the Gate, and complimented them with three Strings of Wampum. By the first he wiped away their Tears for the French that had been slain in the War. By the second he opened their Mouths, that they might speak freely; that is, promised them Freedom of Speech. By the third he cleaned the Matt, on which they were to sit, from the Blood that had been spilt on both Sides: The Compliment was returned by the Jesuit, then they entered the Fort, and were saluted with a general Discharge of all the fire Arms. They were carried to the best Cabin in the Fort, and there entertained with a Feast. The Deputies of the several Nations not being all arrived, the Jesuit, and Monsieur Maricour, passed the Time in visiting and conversing with the French Prisoners. The General Council being at last met, the Jesuit made the following Speech, which I take from the Relation the Five Nations afterwards made of it to the Earl of Bellamont.

"1. I am glad to see the Five Nations, and that some of them went to Canada, notwithstanding Corlear forbid them: I am sorry for the Loss of your People killed by the remote Indians; I condole their Death, and wipe away the Blood by this Belt.

"2. The War Kettle boiled so long, that it would have scalded all the Five Nations had it continued; but now it is overset, and turned upside down, and a firm Peace made.

"3. I now plant the Tree of Peace and Welfare at Onondaga.

"4. Keep fast the Chain you have made with Corlear, for now we have one Heart and one Interest with them; but why is Corlear against your corresponding with us, ought we not to converse together when we are at Peace and in Friendship?

"5. Deliver up the French Prisoners you have, and we shall

deliver not only those of your Nation we have, but all those likewise taken by any of our Allies; and gave a Belt.

"6. I offer myself to you to live with you at Onondaga, to instruct you in the Christian Religion, and to drive away all Sickness, Plagues and Diseases out of your Country, and gave a third Belt.

"7. This last Belt, he said, is from the Rondaxe, or French Indians, to desire Restitution of the Prisoners taken from them."

The Jesuit in the Conclusion said; "Why does not Corlear tell you what passes between the Governor of Canada and him? He keeps you in the Dark, while the Governor of Canada conceals nothing from his Children. Nor does the Governor of Canada claim your Land, as Corlear does."

The General Council immediately rejected the Belt by which the Jesuit offered to stay with them, saying, We have already accepted Corlear's Belt, by which he offers us Pastors to instruct us. Decanesora added, The Jesuits have always deceived us, for while they preached Peace, the French came and knocked us on the Head. To this the Jesuit replied, that if he had known that Corlear intended to send them Pastors, he would not have offered this Belt.

It is to be observed that the Indian Council refused to hear the French, or to give them an Answer, but in Presence of the Commissioners from Albany.

The French Commissioners having assured the Peace with the Five Nations, the Inhabitants of Canada esteemed it the greatest Blessing that could be procured for them from Heaven; for nothing could be more terrible than this last War with the Five Nations. While this War lasted, the Inhabitants eat their Bread in continual Fear and Trembling. No Man was sure, when out of his House, of ever returning to it again. While they laboured in the Fields, they were under perpetual Apprehensions of being killed or seized, and carried to the Indian Country, there to end their Days in cruel Torments. They many Times were forced to neglect both their Seed Time and Harvest. The Landlord often saw all his Land plundered, his Houses burnt, and the whole Country ruined, while they thought their Persons not safe in their Fortifications. In short, all Trade and Business was often at an intire Stand, while Fear, Despair, and Misery appeared in the Faces of the poor Inhabitants.

The French Commissioners carried several of the principal Sachems of the Five Nations back with them, who were received at Montreal with great Joy. They were saluted by a Discharge of all the great Guns round the Place, as they entered. The French Allies took this amiss, and asked if their Governor was entering. They were told, that it was a Compliment paid to the Five Nations, whose Sachems were then entering the Town. We perceive, they replied, that Fear makes the French shew more Respect to their Enemies than Love can make them do to their Friends.

Monsieur de Callieres assembled all the French Allies, (who were then very numerous at Montreal) to make the Exchange of Prisoners, and they delivered the Prisoners they had taken, though the Five Nations had sent none to be exchanged for them. Thus we see a brave People struggle with every Difficulty, till they can get out of it with Honour; and such People always gain Respect, even from their most inveterate Enemies.

I shall finish this Part by observing, that notwithstanding the French Commissioners took all the Pains possible to carry Home the French, that were Prisoners with the Five Nations, and they had full Liberty from the Indians, few of them could be persuaded to return. It may be thought that this was occasioned from the Hardships they had endured in their own Country, under a tyrannical Government and a barren Soil: But this certainly was not the only Reason; for the English had as much Difficulty to persuade the People, that had been taken Prisoners by the French Indians, to leave the Indian Manner of living, though no People enjoy more Liberty, and live in greater Plenty, than the common Inhabitants of New-York do. No Arguments, no Intreaties, nor Tears of their Friends and Relations, could persuade many of them to leave their new Indian Friends and Acquaintance; several of them that were by the Caressings of their Relations persuaded to come Home, in a little Time grew tired of our Manner of living, and run away again to the Indians, and ended their Days with them. On the other Hand, Indian Children have been carefully educated among the English, cloathed and taught, yet, I think, there is not one Instance, that any of these, after they had Liberty to go among their own People, and were come to Age, would remain with the English, but returned to their own Nations, and became as fond of the Indian Manner of Life as those that knew nothing of a civilized Manner of living. What I now tell of Christian Prisoners among Indians, relates not only to what happened at the Conclusion of this War, but has been found true on many other Occasions.

The End of the Second Part.